Happy Birthday, Dennis
Mother

6/25/67

In the Footsteps of Martin Luther

In the Footsteps
of Martin Luther

by

M. A. Kleeberg and Gerhard Lemme

Illustrations, Jacket, and Cover Design
By Alexander Alfs
Translated by Erich Hopka

Concordia Publishing House
St. Louis, Missouri

A translation of *Auf den Lebenswegen Martin Luthers*, by M. A. Kleeberg and Gerhard Lemme
Copyright 1964 by Evangelische Verlagsanstalt GmbH Berlin
Typography by Heinrich Grote

Licensed English Edition
First published 1966
Library of Congress Catalog Card No. 65-26709
Printed in East Germany

Concordia Publishing House, St. Louis, Missouri
Concordia Publishing House Ltd., London, E. C. 1

Moehra

To follow the footsteps of the great figures of history is an enlightening experience. For the decisions of a great life leave their imprint on the environment; it, in turn, reveals the spiritual context in which historic deeds came about. This is the real reason why historical sites are preserved, cared for, and visited.

Martin Luther belongs among the figures that determined, in a very essential way, the history of the German people and the life not only of the Protestant church but of the Christian church as a whole. Luther's religious perception, his catechisms, his translation of the Bible, and his decisive contribution to the development of the German language affect us more than we ourselves realize. For this reason the image of Luther cannot be allowed to grow dim and pale but must be revived afresh with each generation. This requires that we provide care for the Luther sites; above all, it requires that we become acquainted with these historical sites and learn to appreciate them. This book plans to be of assistance in this matter; it fol-

5

lows the footsteps of Martin Luther through the most important events of his life and provides illustrations of the places where he matured and worked.

The village of Moehra lies on the southwestern slope of the Thuringian Forest, north of Salzungen; here the Luther family had resided for a long time. According to an old custom the youngest son always inherited the farm. The other sons usually had to find their living elsewhere. Consequently Hans Luther, Martin's father, with his young wife and a small son moved to Eisleben. Here his second son was born on November 10, 1483. He was baptized the next day and called Martin, the name of the saint for that day.

But the work in Eisleben was hard and the pay poor, so in the early summer of 1484 Hans Luther decided to settle in Mansfeld. At first he worked there as an ordinary miner. Luther himself once said, "My father in his younger years was a poor pick-and-shovel man; my mother carried all her firewood home on her back." However, later Luther's father joined one of the many associations that were organized then to exploit the copper mines. Together with a fellow citizen he was able to lease a foundry. Eventually he had a share in at least eight mines and three foundries. Even at that he did not become exactly rich; however, it was always possible for him to make a living for his large family, which in 1505 consisted of four sons and four daughters. It was of course not without prudence, hard work, and a good deal of thrift that he was able to provide for them.

Martin Luther started school very young. In 1488 he entered the town school in Mansfeld to learn reading, writing, singing, and Latin. Latin was the most important subject. Whoever at that time wanted to get on in the world had to master late-medieval Latin. Singing was taught because the boys' voices were needed for the church services. Luther acquired considerable knowledge in this

Alsleben, the St. Cecilia town church and the old town hall

field, a knowledge which he later was able to use to good advantage in the composition of tunes and texts for hymns.

Discipline in school was stern, just as it was in the parental home. On account of a nut his mother once beat him till he bled, and in school he was whipped with a rod fifteen times one morning. He must have been thinking of these educational methods when he later said, "The rod must have an apple next to it." He meant to say that love and kindness must go hand in hand with the necessary firmness. Luther's parents were strict and had only meager skill in training children, but Luther recognized their kindheartedness and thanked them for it all his life. His letters to them show this in various ways. On February 15, 1530, and May 20, 1531, he wrote to his mother and father shortly before they died and signed the letters with a frank and honest "Your dear son Martin Luther."

In the home of his parents the piety of late-medieval Catholicism held sway. The saints played the main role, and the devil had his finger in every pie. Christ was regarded primarily as the judge of the world, as may be seen, for instance, in a representation now in the city church of Wittenberg. This work, which originated toward the end of the 15th century, had earlier hung on the north wall of the city church. Even in later years Luther could not rid himself entirely of this image of Christ and once confessed : "Even today I cannot look at my Lord Jesus with as happy a face as He would want, because they filled my head with that pestilential teaching which pictured God as angry and Christ as a judge." Superstition, a belief in witches, devils, and saints stifled the glad tidings of man's salvation. When Martin Luther as a young student was on his way from Mansfeld to Erfurt and was caught in a heavy storm, he did not call on God or the Lord Christ but appealed to the patron saint of the miners, from whose ranks he had come. To her he vowed, "Saint Anne, help, I want to become a monk!"

In the spring of 1497 Hans Luther sent his son Martin to Magdeburg to a school run by the Brethren of the Common Life. Their intensely subjective piety, which emphasized above all a humble attitude toward God, seems not to have made a marked impression on Luther. He related later that, when he was in Magdeburg, he had seen Prince William of Anhalt, who had joined the Franciscan Order in 1473, going down the highway begging "bread for God" as a mendicant friar would. "He had starved and castigated himself so that he looked like a picture of death, nothing but skin and bones. Whoever looked at him savored devotion and had to be ashamed of his own station in life."

At Easter time in 1498 Martin Luther returned to Mansfeld. His parents now sent him to relatives in Eisenach, "his beloved city," as he later called it. There they had hoped he would be in better hands than in Magdeburg, but this was not to be. His rela-

Aschersleben
St. Stephen's Church
erected in the 14th century

The cathedral in Magdeburg

St. Mary's Church in Magdeburg

The city hall in Plauen

tives could not furnish him free lodging, and so, for the time being, at least, he must have found a bed in one of the infirmaries or in a school which at that time had sleeping quarters for poor students. As in Magdeburg, he had to beg for a living —as a choir boy singing in the streets. It was not until his singing caught the attention of a matron in a church service that his affairs took a turn for the better. In the home of a well-to-do businessman named Schalbe he received free board, for which he had to take little Henry, a son of the family, to school and supervise his homework. Apparently he also found lodging in the home of Ursula Cotta, whose maiden name was Schalbe. There he met people who lived by faith. The Cotta family maintained connections with the Franciscan friars, who had a small monastery at the foot of the Wartburg. Martin Luther was now drawn into this circle of devout people. The St. George parish school also made a significant contribution to his education. Here he became really sure of himself in Latin. He learned to deliver Latin speeches and compose Latin verses. He retained a fond memory of his schoolmaster Trebonius, who always took off his little cap when he entered the classroom. "For, sitting here," he said, "among these young students, there is many a one whom God can later make into a mayor, a chancellor, a highly learned doctor, or a governor."

In Eisenach Luther learned what he could. Then the beautiful years in this city came to an end. At seventeen he was permitted to enroll in the University of Erfurt. Meanwhile his father had worked his way up to where he could afford a university education for his son. He wanted to make a lawyer out of him in the sure hope that, after graduation and through the efforts of the Count of Mansfeld, he would find a good position for his son. Even a rich bride had already been selected for Luther!

Munich, old city hall, the former gate to the city

Scala burial vaults in Verona

The cathedral in Florence

Before beginning professional study, it was necessary to complete a basic course of study in the seven "liberal arts," divided into the *trivium* (grammar, logic, rhetoric) and the *quadrivium* (music, arithmetic, geometry, and astronomy). The *trivium* terminated with a bachelor's examination and the *quadrivium* with a master's. Even the bachelor was a member of the university faculty. If he continued his study, he was obligated also to lecture and conduct recitations. After this "basic course" one was allowed to specialize in theology, medicine, or jurisprudence. So Martin Luther also began with the "liberal arts." He had to live in a students' hostel or dormitory, where the studies, the daily routine, and religious exercises were regulated and controlled in every detail. Out on the street he wore a kind of gown with a barret, as did all students, to indicate to everyone that he was a student. In 1505 he became a master of

The cathedral in Siena

liberal arts and began to study law. Now his father began to dream of the brilliant career in store for his son.

In midsemester Martin Luther paid a visit to his parents in Mansfeld and was caught in that severe storm during which a bolt of lightning struck the ground next to him. In deep anxiety he vowed to become a monk, for what kind of judgment would have awaited him had the bolt struck him! What if he had been summoned before the Judge of the world, unprepared and unreconciled by the church's means of grace! It was his terror of that judgment that drove him into the monastery. On July 16th he invited his friends to a farewell gathering, at which he said, "You are seeing me for the last time." This promise he kept. His horrified friends could not persuade him otherwise. To be sure, for a long time he had been convinced that the grace of God could be earned best by living as

13

a monk. And so on July 17, 1505, he went, as though called by God Himself and despite the protestations of his inner self, and placed himself under the strict discipline of the Augustinian Eremites. At first his father would not consent to it but later, in a second letter, he gave his permission, though with a heavy heart. At first Luther had to spend a waiting period in the monastery inn. This time was meant to be used in self-examination. Then he was received into the novitiate, the actual probation period for the monastic life. During this time he had to decide whether he was both mentally and physically fit to carry out the strict regulations of the order.

He was willing to submit to every monastic regulation. He was not ashamed to beg for the monastery in the villages around Erfurt, and he observed the spiritual exercises, the vigils, and the fasting with scrupulous care. However, neither his study of the Bible nor the many monastic rituals were able to give him that peace for which he so greatly longed. Even the day on which he was actually accepted into the order, when he received the so-called monk's baptism, contributed nothing to his peace of mind. Profession—the taking of the eternally binding vow in the Augustinian Order—was called monk's baptism because it was believed to have the same salutary effect as Baptism itself. Like many monks before him, Luther had now taken the solemn vow, folded his hands over the book containing the rules of the Augustinian Order, and said, "I, Brother Martin, do make this profession and promise obedience ..." The prescribed ceremonies had been performed as always, and a new consecrated cowl had been given to him, but what he so greatly desired did not occur. Even after profession he had not become a new person! In the cell which now had been assigned to him he eagerly studied, prayed much, and so prepared himself for the ordination which his prior had determined he was to receive. In April 1507 he was ordained to the priesthood in the cathedral in Erfurt. On Sunday, May 2, 1507, he was permitted to say mass for the first

The city hall in Siena

The Pantheon in Rome

Cologne, Great St. Martin

time. He did it with fear and trembling. Later he wrote concerning it, "When I celebrated my first mass in Erfurt, I nearly died, for there was no faith on my part. My only concern was to be personally worthy and not a sinner, and not to omit anything from the mass with its signs of the cross and pageantry."

Luther's father came for the occasion with friends and acquaintances and made a large gift of twenty florins to the monastery. When Luther asked him why he had so bitterly opposed his wish to become a monk, even though his son had heard God's voice in the storm, the father asked him if he might not have heard the devil's voice. When Luther tried to defend himself, his father cut him short with: "You learned people, haven't you ever read in Holy Scripture that one should honor father and mother?" Luther never forgot these words of his father. They continued to trouble him, and later he became increasingly concerned about whether God had really called him to be a monk.

At first, of course, he earnestly and zealously devoted himself to the monastic life, that "fine peaceful life." Whatever the monastery demanded : prayer, meditations, silence, he fulfilled with greatest care. Each week he went to confession, but it was not able to help him. The peace he sought would not come to him. The forgiveness pronounced to him was based on his doing, the deeds of man. "May the penance and the good works which you have done and still will do contribute to the remission of your sins, to the multiplication of your merits, and to your reward of eternal life." Those were the words he heard in the absolution. Also he was constantly beset by the question, "Is God's grace meant also for me ?" Time and again he experienced for himself the truth of Paul's words : "The good I want to do I do not do, but the evil I do not want to do I do." And so his doubts became more intense. "I know of a person," he said of himself, "who claims to have often suffered such torture, torture so great and so fiendish, that no tongue can declare it, no pen describe it, and no one believe it who has not experienced it himself ... Then God seems gruesome and angry, and together with Him the whole creation. There is no escape, no comfort, neither within nor without, but only indictment from everywhere. In such a moment one cannot believe that one could ever be saved ; all one knows is that punishment has not yet come to an end." What the message about Christ, the Savior and Redeemer, meant to Luther can be understood only in the light of these shattering experiences.

In the year 1508 Luther was called, apparently upon the recommendation of the vicar-general of the Augustinian Order, Dr. John von Staupitz, to the University of Wittenberg, recently founded by the elector, Frederick the Wise. He was commissioned by the prior of his order to lecture on the philosophy of Aristotle in the faculty

Castle and fortress of Marienberg in Wuerzburg

of liberal arts. He moved into the Augustinian monastery at Wittenberg and was thrown into personal contact with John von Staupitz. This event was of extraordinary importance for him, for he chose this venerable man for his father confessor. In answer to the question that tormented him, whether he had been elected by God to eternal salvation, John von Staupitz referred him again and again to the wounds of Christ, that is, to the Savior who had died for him. Thus he told him: "Why do you want to worry yourself with your thoughts? Take hold of Christ's wounds and look at the most sacred blood that was shed for our sins—mine, yours, and those of all people. Remember 'My sheep hear my voice,' (John 10:27)." So Staupitz stood by him in all his spiritual struggles to the best of his ability, but, of course, he could not help him find his inner peace. Not only teaching duties kept Luther occupied during this year. The young teacher himself attended lectures in theology.

Miltenberg on the Main

The city hall in Michelstadt in Odenwald

In 1509 Luther was back again in Erfurt to take charge of the theological education of the monks and to continue his own theological studies at Erfurt University. During this time he studied Greek and also Hebrew, for he sensed that one could not in every case depend on the Vulgate, the Latin translation of the Bible.

In 1510 Luther journeyed to Rome in the interest of his order. Probably he had been assigned as a travel companion to the actual official delegate. The order considered this journey necessary because serious quarrels were threatening its unity. As far as we can tell, their itinerary took them from Nuremberg to Ulm, then through upper Swabia and western Switzerland over the Septimer Pass toward Milan (where they crossed the Apennines is not clear), from Florence along the old imperial highway through Siena and Ronciglione to Rome. Since the negotiations in Rome progressed rather slowly, Luther had an opportunity to learn to know the city and its churches quite well. He was thoroughly disillusioned in his hope to find peace by making a "general confession" there, for it was precisely in Rome that church life had become a business transaction in many ways.

In late January or early February the two friars again left the "holy city," perhaps starting back on the same road on which they had come. Then they probably went from Florence through Bologna and San Benedetto Po to Verona, from there on toward the Brenner peak, still deeply covered by snow. After they had negotiated the Brenner Pass and left Innsbruck, they traveled in a westerly direction to Scharnitz Pass and journeyed through Partenkirchen and Schongau to Augsburg, and finally in a northerly direction to Erfurt. Luther returned to Germany filled with grave doubts. He was thankful that he had learned to know Rome from personal observation.

He was not to remain in Erfurt much longer. Luther broke away from the monastery at Erfurt as a result of internal disagreements in his order. He had opposed the majority opinion and sided with the vicar-general, Dr. von Staupitz. And so, probably late in the summer of 1511, he had to retreat to Wittenberg, certainly with the approval of the vicar-general, for without it he could not have been admitted to the monastery there. May 2 – 8, 1512, he was in Cologne, at a general chapter of his order. There the assembled delegates of the reformed Augustinian monasteries elected him subprior, that is, assistant superior of the Wittenberg monastery. At the same time he was placed in charge of the monastery's school for the friars.

The year 1512 brought Luther an important decision. Upon the insistence of Staupitz he finished his theological studies and received the degree of doctor of theology. This gave him the right to become the professor of Biblical theology at the University of Wittenberg and lecture on the Bible. The graduation took place

Castle Homberg on the Neckar

with great solemnity in October of 1512. The elector, who hoped his newly founded university would greatly profit by having Luther, bore the cost of the festivities.

Three days after his graduation Luther became a member of the faculty of Wittenberg University, replacing Dr. Staupitz, who had given up his chair of Biblical theology.

Luther began to lecture. His interpretation of the Psalms and of the epistles to the Romans and to the Galatians attracted attention. The students sensed that Luther had something to offer them. Little by little he came upon the Reformation insight that God accepts us sinners as His children for Christ's sake. What man does cannot justify him before God. Only faith which relies on the merits of Christ can save a person and rescue him from God's final judgment. "The heart of a Christian is a precious tablet which has written on it that it is saved by Christ," he said later. But this understanding was still insecure and shaky: God was still an avenging God to

21

Weinheim on the mountain highway

Luther, demanding all. Luther had to experience that he fell far short of this requirement and that all the church's means, spiritual exercises, praying and fasting, were of no help. He found no help until one day he paused again at the passage concerning the righteousness of God : "For in it [the Gospel] the righteousness which is valid before God is revealed, a righteousness based on faith and for faith; as it is written : 'The righteous shall live on account of his faith.'" Luther meditated on Paul's words : Is it God's *avenging* righteousness that is revealed in the Gospel ? "Astonished and bewildered I asked myself this question : Time and again I knocked at Paul's door in a feverish attempt to understand and unfold what he really meant in this passage." And then the scales fell from his eyes. The righteousness of which Paul here speaks is not God's avenging justice, the righteousness of requirements, but the righteousness which God gives to him who clings to Christ in faith. He wrote to George Spenlein on April 18, 1516: "Therefore, my dear

22

City of Kronach with Fort Rosenberg above it

brother, learn to know Christ, yes, the Crucified. Learn to praise Him, to despair of yourself, and to say to Him: Lord Jesus, You are my righteousness, but I am Your sin; You took what is mine and gave me what is Yours. You took upon Yourself what You were not and gave me what I was not." Luther said of himself when he was given this insight: "I felt as if I had been born completely anew again and had stepped though open doors into Paradise. At once the whole Bible looked different to me ... The more I had hated the words 'righteousness of God' in the past, the dearer and sweeter they seemed now. So that passage of Paul's has truly become the gate to Paradise for me." From his words we sense the profound relief he felt. Even though in later years deep struggles were to shake him time and again, he now had found the foundation on which he could stand and to which he could always return: God's grace which comes to us through Jesus Christ, which we can only accept, and which we ourselves cannot earn.

23

Old bridge over the Main at Kulmbach

In May of 1515 an event of importance for Luther's future work occurred: At a general chapter of his order in Gotha he was appointed district vicar of the Augustinian Eremites. This put him in charge of the ten cloisters in Meissen and Thuringia—Wittenberg, Dresden, Herzberg, Gotha, Langensalza, Nordhausen, Sangerhausen, Erfurt, Magdeburg, and Neustadt on the Orla. Now he was in a position to spread the seed of the Gospel through correspondence with the individual brothers of his order and with the monasteries, as well as through the visitation he made to Dresden, Erfurt, Gotha, Langensalza, and Erfurt in the latter half of April 1516.

At first Luther did not realize how revolutionary his new find was. Through study and interpretation of the Scriptures he deepened it. Then one day the hour came in which his new discovery became a matter of public notice too. This happened first in the indulgence controversy.

24

What does indulgence mean? The priest after absolution imposes on the penitent a penance for sin, perhaps an offering, a pilgrimage, specified prayers. But the church already has a treasure of good works which were done by Christ and the saints. They had done more than was required for their justification. From this "store" a person who has sinned can, in exchange for a corresponding offering of money, acquire enough to satisfy the obligations of his penance. This is what happened in the indulgence transaction.

In those days it had long become a money racket. It was thought one could buy one's salvation by this means. In fact, indulgence could be had even for the dead. "When you drop the money in, the soul will leap to heaven, purged from sin," cried John Tetzel, who sold the letters of indulgence. He had set up shop in nearby Jueterbog after Frederick the Wise had refused to let him stay in Saxony. The elector had his

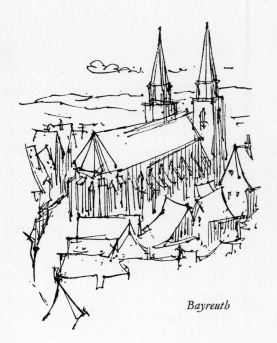

Bayreuth

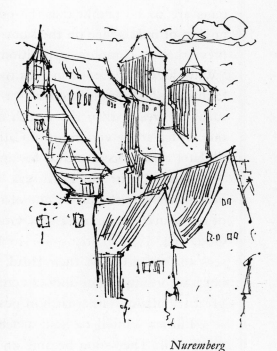

Nuremberg

25

own relics and his own indulgence business and wanted to keep the money in his territory.

While hearing confession Luther encountered the utter confusion that was caused by the indulgence traffic. The faithful to whom Luther had to deny absolution demanded it because they had bought letters of indulgence. And so his experience as a father confessor in connection with the sale of indulgences developed into a burning issue of conscience for him and forced him to act. On October 31, 1517, Luther nailed his theses concerning the indulgence traffic on the door of the Castle Church in Wittenberg. The 95 Theses, which at first had been intended only for learned circles, spread very rapidly through all of Germany, "as though angels had been their couriers." They still contained some genuinely Catholic statements. Luther had not yet thought of abolishing indulgences in principle, and he still attributed good intentions to the pope. "Christians are to be taught that the pope in no way intends to put the buying of indulgence on the same level with the works of charity." Nevertheless, complete opposition was already becoming apparent. "Why doesn't the pope use his own money rather than that of the faithful poor to build the basilica of St. Peter at least? His fortune today is greater than the wealth of the richest Crassus." Here Luther struck at the very heart of Catholic piety even though it was not till later that it became clear to him. Let us quote three theses here: "(1) When Christ our Lord says 'repent,' He means that the entire life of believers should be one of repentance. (62) The true treasure of the church is the most holy Gospel about the glory and grace of God. (94, 95) Christians are to be admonished that they should seek to follow Christ, their Head, through chastisement, death, and hell; accordingly they should confidently expect to enter heaven in great tribulation rather than in peace and security."

Luther wanted to hold a debate over the theses, but nothing came of it. They soon became known in all of Germany, yes, even

Nuremberg, according to an engraving by Merian

far beyond. At a chapter of his order in Heidelberg in 1518 Luther
again defended his desire for a reformation. For this he had prepared new theses. Even though the professors opposed him, he
gained many of the students. Here he coined the sentence: "The
theologian of glory calls the bad good and the good bad; but the
theologian of the cross calls things by their right names: sinners
are good because they are loved (by God); they are not loved (by
God) because they are good." Now the pope summoned Luther to
a heresy trial in Rome. The elector and the university opposed this
and managed to get a hearing for Luther in 1518 before Cardinal
Cajetan in Augsburg.

The cardinal demanded that he recant. Luther appealed to
Scripture. He barely escaped the arrest that had been planned for
him. What he had written to his friend George Spalatin on August 8,
before starting the journey, turned out to be true: ". . . Finally I ask
you not to be sad or worried about me. The Lord who sent the test
will at the same time provide a way out."

27

*The tower of Perlach in Augsburg and
the Renaissance city hall by Elijah Holl*

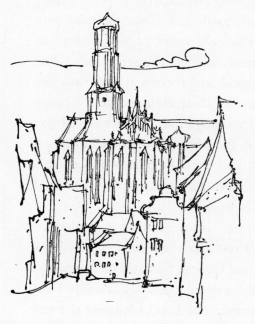

Augsburg, St. Ulrich and Afra

Luther appealed to the pope in every manner possible. The Saxon nobleman Charles von Miltitz, who served as papal chamberlain, tried to settle the matter. But when he came to the Saxon court with many letters demanding that Luther be handed over, he sensed very quickly that public opinion in Germany was on Luther's side and that, if he wished to accomplish anything, he would have to proceed in an amicable manner. After von Miltitz had presented the elector with a gold rose blessed by the pope, the elector gave permission for holding a consultation at Altenburg. There it was agreed that Luther would keep quiet in public from now on if the opponents would resolve to do the same. But Professor Eck from Ingolstadt broke the silence and attacked Luther. That is why Luther accompanied the Wittenberg professor Bodenstein von Carlstadt to the disputation at Leipzig to which the latter had been invited. Eck renewed his attack on Luther. Luther

Arnstadt, the Ried gate, the St. James tower, and the Guenther mill

defended himself and declared, among other things, that the councils of the church could err and had erred. Now Luther's rupture with the pope became an open one, for all men to see; but he had simultaneously, through the disputation at Leipzig, become the most popular man in Germany.

Now he wrote his four major Reformation documents: "An Address to the Christian Nobility of the German Nation Concerning the Reform of Christendom," "The Babylonian Captivity of the Church," "Christian Liberty," and "Treatise on Good Works." Sparing no one, he uncovered the evils of his time and church and also indicated ways to reform the church in both its head and members.

The papal bull secured by Eck as a result of his report on the Leipzig disputation and threatening Luther with excommunication unless he recanted in sixty days met with no response in Germany. Even though Luther's writings had been burned in some West-German cities, Luther in return made his position clear by burning the papal bull on December 10, 1520, in front of the Elster gate of Wittenberg, in the presence of many students, and by hurling the books of the Roman canon law into the fire. The latter was even more serious. Now all bridges between him and Rome were burned.

On January 3, 1521, Luther was put under the Great Excommunication. In spite of this the German estates, with Frederick the Wise at the head, managed to get Luther a hearing at the Diet of Worms. The emperor promised safe-conduct for him, and he kept his word even though Luther had been excommunicated. Luther's journey to Worms turned into a triumphal procession, which plainly showed that the entire nation was interested in this controversy.

On April 16, 1521, at 10 o'clock in the morning, Luther entered Worms, guarded by a hundred horsemen and surrounded by large crowds. On April 17, in the afternoon at four, Luther appeared for the first time before the diet assembled in the episcopal palace, the quarters of the emperor. He was accompanied by his friend and legal adviser, Jerome Schurf. Dr. John, the archiepiscopal officer from Trier, asked Luther the three famous questions: Whether the books before the diet and others bearing his name were his, whether he intended to defend them further, or whether he was prepared to recant. He was grudgingly given one day for reflection. But at its end he gave a clear answer: "Unless I am proved wrong on the basis of testimony of Scripture or by clear rational arguments, I remain bound by the Scripture passages to which I have referred. My conscience is a captive to God's word; for I do not believe just the pope or the councils, since it is plain that they have often erred and contradicted themselves. I cannot and will not retract anything because it is neither safe nor advisable to do anything against one's conscience. God help me. Amen."

Fulda, St. Michel's

For two more days and with the utmost kindness they tried to get Luther to change his mind. But he stood firm. The emperor offered to maintain the safe-conduct provided Luther did not teach, preach, or write on the way to Wittenberg. But the elector informed Luther that somewhere along the way he was going to have him "locked up." Luther left Worms to go back to Wittenberg through Frankfurt, Hersfeld, and Eisenach. On the way back he was advised to turn off the main highway. He visited his relatives in Moehra, spent the night there, and preached under the open sky. Near the Altenstein castle his companion Amsdorf saw several horsemen coming out of the woods. Luther grabbed his Greek New Testament and his Hebrew Bible, just in case. Brother Patzenheimer, one of Luther's companions, who had no idea what was afoot, leaped from the wagon and hid in the bushes. The riders gruffly asked the driver whether it was Luther he had with him. He quickly admitted

31

Frankfurt on the Main

it was. They pulled Luther down from the wagon, dragged him away with them, and made him run along beside them. Not until the wagon was out of sight, did they reveal their identity. They set him on a horse, and after riding back and forth for hours he finally arrived at the Wartburg around eleven at night. The castle captain, von Berlepsch, received him very warmly. Luther had to take off his cowl, dress like a knight, and let his hair grow out. Not until he had grown a beard and his tonsure had disappeared was he permitted to appear before others, now as Squire George, for he was outlawed and put under the imperial ban on May 25th.

Luther knew how to put his "forced vacation" at the Wartburg to good use. He began the work that so greatly influenced the life of the German nation and the Protestant church: the translation of the Holy Scriptures. To be sure, there were translations of the Bible into German already available, but these were awkward, wooden, and lacked vitality. Two examples will be enough to illustrate this. In a German Bible published before Luther Psalm 23:4 reads: "Your rod and Your staff, the same have comforted me"; another translated: "Your rod and Your crutch," and a Meistersinger even rendered it: "Your broom and Your cudgel." On the other hand, how nicely Luther puts it: "Your rod and staff comfort me." The old Bible had translated Psalm 50:15: "Call on me in the day of tribulation, and I redeem you, and you honor Me." How close to life, how alive, and dynamic does this become with Luther: "Call upon me in trouble, and I will save you, and you will praise Me." Luther wanted to translate so that everyone could understand him: "You must not ask the Latin grammar how to talk German, as these fools do; ask the housewife, the children in the alley, and the common man in the market place, observe how they talk and then translate accordingly;

Frankfurt on the Main, Hall Court

Lorsch, the cloister porch, A.D. 830

33

then they will understand and realize you are talking German to them."

What drove Luther to this work was his desire to make Holy Scripture, as source of all knowledge of faith, accessible to every person in the land. Although he had no intention of creating a standard language, his translation made him, in fact, the father of a uniform literary German, for his Bible was widely distributed, read, and understood by all who spoke German in any dialect. Many of the expressions from his Bible became a part of the common idiom of the German people.

Luther was a master of language. Over and over again he found new words to bring out the finer points of a text: "way," "road," "path," "footpath," "highway !" What a fitting contrast: "the gate of heaven" but "the door of the cottage !" How easy to remember are the alliterations he used, like "thorns and thistles," "weary and worn," or "let your light" ! How he labored and chiseled away to do ever better justice to the meaning of the Biblical text ! In 1524 Luther translated Psalm 37:7 : "Stand still before God and let him handle you," later (1531) : "Wait for the Lord and set your hope on Him," and finally in 1541 : "Be at peace in the Lord and set your hope on Him."

Much more could be said about the richness of Luther's vocabulary, but this would go beyond the scope of our book. In any event, Luther's language was a determining factor in the important language development taking place in that period and formed the basis of modern High German prose; it enriched the language for centuries to come. Luther worked with great zeal. Working six hours each day between the end of December 1521 and the end of February 1522, he wrote a brilliant German translation of the New Testament. Since it was published in September, it was called the "September Bible." Although it was still very expensive, it was sold out in a few days. Before long reprints appeared in great number.

34

Zwingenberg Castle near Heidelberg

Meanwhile the world had become caught in a turmoil. Ferment and unrest appeared everywhere. In the theological realm Carlstadt and his followers tried to reform the church by force. In the Lord's Supper both bread and wine were to be distributed to the communicants, monasteries were to be abandoned, monks were to be permitted to marry, and images were to disappear from the churches. Tumults arose, and monks saying mass were pelted with stones.

Luther realized that the work which he had begun as an act of faith was being misrepresented and threatened. For this reason he secretly left the Wartburg to set things right at Wittenberg. On December 4th he came to Professor Amsdorf's house. He looked like a traveling stranger and was not immediately recognized by the people in the house. He stayed in Wittenberg only five days and returned to the Wartburg as quietly as he had come. He recorded his impressions and concerns in a document which appeared soon

35

Graefenhainichen,
the town of Paul Gerhardt

after he returned to the Wartburg: "Admonition to all Christians to Beware of Riot and Rebellion." He had already stated his position in a letter he wrote to Spalatin on January 16, 1521: "I would not want anyone to contend for the Gospel with violence and bloodshed. The world was overcome through the Word, through the Word the church was saved, through the Word it will be restored. Just as the Antichrist started without violence, so he will be crushed without violence, through the Word." The disturbances in Wittenberg continued. Now Luther forsook his place of refuge in the Wartburg for good and, against the will of the elector, returned to Wittenberg. He left on March 1st; from Borna he wrote him a letter on March 5th which reveals not only Luther's frankness but also the boldness of his faith. In it he said: "This is being written to Your Grace with the thought in mind that Your Grace should know that I am coming to Wittenberg under far greater protection than that of the elector's. I also do not intend to seek protection from Your Grace. Yes, I am convinced I would protect Your Grace more than Your Grace could protect me. Furthermore, if I knew Your Grace could and would protect me, I would not come. The sword should not and cannot give help and advice in this matter. Here God must work alone, without man's help and interference. For here it is true: He who believes most protects most. And since I sense that Your Grace's faith is still very weak, I cannot in any way feel that Your Grace is the man that could protect or rescue me."

The uptown tower
in Graefenhainichen, erected in 1448

Luther preached for eight days straight every single morning in the Wittenberg parish church. His principle that the Word must do it proved correct; quiet and order were restored. "In summary: I will preach it, I will speak it, I will write it, but I will not force or coerce anyone. Faith wants to be free and not be forced or accepted under compulsion."

Not only did he establish peace in Wittenberg; he also

Naumburg, the St. Mary's gate,
part of the city's old fortifications

preached in the market place of Zwickau, and elsewhere, and exhorted the people to be peaceful and sensible. But that was not enough. A new form of liturgy was needed, one which would correspond to the knowledge of faith gained from Holy Scriptures. In a sermon at the dedication of the Castle Church in Torgau he told how he wanted the church service to be understood: as a dialog with God through His Word and through the believers' prayers and hymns of praise. Hymns, prayers, and sermons, all should be in German. It was for the Protestant church services above all, that he composed hymns such as: "A Mighty Fortress," "From Depths of Woe," "May God Bestow on Us His Grace." Many of these were paraphrases of the Psalms.

On October 29, 1525, in a church service in Wittenberg, at which Luther preached and George Roerer led the liturgy, the entire liturgy was sung in German for the first time. This was of decisive significance, for now the congregation could fully participate in the whole service.

The people could now sing in church! What great force streamed forth from the sung Word! It has been said, and rightly so, that hymns did even more to spread the Reformation than the preached and printed Word. What a wealth of possibilities for instructing children presented themselves after Luther had produced his Small Catechism! The Large Catechism appeared earlier. The people were made familiar with and enriched by Biblical thought, and at the same time gained a better knowledge of their ancestral language. But how did Luther come to write his catechisms? He was driven to it by a need which existed in the parishes. The church visitation which had been carried out in the electorate of Saxony and elsewhere disclosed a shocking picture of spiritual ignorance. Quite often the people were no longer Catholic and had discarded Catholic customs, but they had in no way grasped that the new evangelical freedom imposed on them a great moral responsibility. In addition

Naumburg with the church of St. Maurice, the cathedral, and the church of St. Wenceslas

to this, the old property of the church, which should have been available for the support of the ministers and of Christian education, was considered as freehold property claimed by anybody who could wield enough power. Many suffered under this state of affairs. So representations were made to Elector Frederick the Wise to have him take personal charge of the Reformation in his territories. On May 1, 1525, Spalatin had written to the elector, requesting him to ask all clergy and monasteries from now on to arrange the church service in conformity with the pure Word of God and to put an end to all unwarranted practices. We do not know whether the elector ever read this letter. He was a sick man and had been confined to his castle in Lochau since early 1525. When his condition grew worse, his physician sent for Spalatin. An attempt was also made to bring Luther, but he did not see the elector alive anymore. Words of comfort from the Bible, written out by Spalatin the previous night, were read to Frederick the Wise. The elector expressly requested and re-

39

ceived both bread and wine in the Holy Communion. By this gesture he declared his faith in the work of the Reformation, to which he had extended his protection many times, just as he had to Luther. On May 5th he closed his eyes in death, but not before he had asked forgiveness of those around him.

Luther preached the funeral sermon based on 1 Thessalonians 4:13-18. He remembered his shrewd protector many times during his later life. The visitations were now resumed by the successor of Frederick the Wise, John the Steadfast. In February 1527 a visitation was conducted in the Wittenberg district by Melanchthon, the lawyer Schurf, and two laymen of the nobility; then in July of 1527 it was undertaken in several districts of Thuringia by Melanchthon, Myconius from Gotha, Menius from Erfurt, and by three lay councilors of the prince.

Based on the findings of the visitations a document appeared at Eastertime 1528 entitled: "Instructions of the Visitors to the Clergy in the Electorate of Saxony." During the visitations, which still went on for many years, the clergy were examined in Christian doctrine and understanding. They were instructed how to administer the office of the ministry properly and how to exercise pastoral care. At meetings of family heads the parishes were asked for their opinion of their clergy, and the assets of the parishes were examined and officially established. At the same time an attempt was made to correct the evils which had arisen in the parishes. Luther also occasionally took part in these visitations. The Small Catechism and the Large Catechism are the fruit of the visitations. Luther wanted to give pastors and fathers a tool for their own Christian edification, as well as for the Christian instruction of the parishes and the households entrusted to them. All his life Luther called himself a student of the catechism. Even though I am "a doctor and preacher," he confessed in 1530 in a new edition of the Large Catechism, "I am like a child that is being taught the catechism. I repeat word for

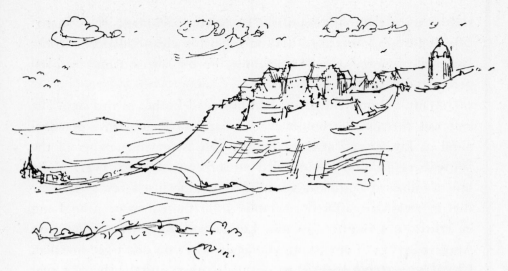

Neuenburg at Freyburg on the Unstrut

word, morning and evening, if I have time, the Ten Command-
ments, the Lord's Prayer, Psalms, etc.; I have to remain a child
and a student of the catechism, and I am glad to be one."

In June of 1525 Luther married Katherine von Bora, one of
those nuns who had left the Nimbschen convent and for whom he
had made a special effort to find suitable marriages. Deep and serious thought went into his decision to marry before it finally became
a reality. "If this monk," said Luther's friend, Jerome Schurf, "gets
married, the whole world and the devil himself will laugh, and he
will undo all he has done so far." But Luther wrote to Spalatin:
"When I got married, the world laughed, and so I hope the angels
are pleased and the devils weep." Katherine was "worth more to
him than the entire kingdom of France." The available letters of
Luther to his wife bear witness to the happy relationship in which
they lived.

Pastor Bugenhagen of Wittenberg performed the wedding cere-
mony in the former cloister in which Luther lived. Luther's mar-

41

riage marked the founding of the Protestant parsonage in Germany. The Reformer's marriage not only gave a clear sanction for the Evangelical clergy's leading a family life but also became its ideal prototype.

Many a Protestant pastor had preceded Luther in this step. The first was provost Bartholomew Bernhardi of Kemberg, a personal pupil of Luther and at the same time an esteemed member of the Wittenberg faculty. He married already on May 30, 1521. Many others followed Bernhardi's lead. To mention just a few : Matthew Zell in Strasbourg, Dr. Pomeranus John Bugenhagen, John Lang in Erfurt, and George Spalatin. Luther had written to Spalatin on April 10, 1525 : "I am asking you again why you don't get married. I have been trying so hard to persuade others to take the step that I almost feel like getting married myself. But our enemies will not quit condemning marriage ; their wiseacres joke about it every day." What blessings have flowed from Luther's home ! What a blessing the Protestant parsonage has been to the German lands and other countries ! How many important leaders have come from a Protestant parsonage !

Luther and his home became the focal point of a large circle of people. Someone was always coming or going. Yet Katherine, by her hard work, prudence, and ingenuity, managed to provide the means which such a large household required. She succeeded in making the cloister snug and comfortable. Every room was full of life. Today only a few things look as they did at that time.

In the year 1527 Wittenberg was threatened with a plague epidemic. Because of this danger the university was moved to Jena and later to Schlieben near Wittenberg. It was not until April 1528 that the university returned to Wittenberg. Luther, however, had stayed, in spite of the elector's urgent plea that he should move with his wife and child to Jena. He wanted to keep Luther safe for the work of the Reformation. To be sure, Luther was concerned

Freyburg on the Unstrut

about the safety of his wife, who was expecting another child. But just now he could not bring himself to leave Wittenberg, for he felt God had placed him there. Bugenhagen, who made such a significant contribution to the Reformation in the North, stayed bravely at his side. Luther said of him (Bugenhagen was his father confessor): "When I was troubled, Pomeranus [Bugenhagen] often gave me comfort at this table . . . To me it was a deep comfort, as though it were the voice of an angel, so firmly was it fixed in my heart . . ." In order to be readily available to Luther, Pomeranus, together with his family, moved into Luther's house, for it was just then that Luther was plagued by deep inner conflicts. He adhered to what he had written on October 26, 1516, to John Lang during another plague epidemic: "You advise me . . . to flee. But why? I hope that the world will not go under even if Brother Martin does. If the epidemic grows worse, I shall have the brothers, of course, spread out around in the country. But I have been placed here by an order, and only if the order changes, am I free to leave."

In 1529 Luther met with Zwingli in Marburg for a colloquy on the fundamentals of faith. But no understanding was reached with the Swiss reformer. The main point of contention was the doctrine of the Lord's Supper. This was the main reason why the negotiations ran aground. For Zwingli the Lord's Supper was a meal in remembrance of Christ. For Luther it involved Christ's bodily presence in the elements of the sacrament. And so that great Protestant alliance did not materialize which might have altered the entire course of Reformation history.

In the meantime Emperor Charles V was preparing a new blow for the Protestants. He called for a new diet at Augsburg and promised that everything would be done according to law and justice. This is why the Saxon elector, John the Steadfast, accepted the invitation, but first he called his theologians Luther, Melanchthon, Justus Jonas, and Bugenhagen to Torgau to hammer out a position

Freyburg on the Unstrut, the market place with the city church, the city hall, and the house (right) in which Luther spent the night in 1522

to be taken at Augsburg. It was there that the so-called Torgau Articles were worked out, articles which were revised again and again, since the emperor kept them waiting so long for the actual convening of the diet. Melanchthon tried to reach a compromise with the Catholics. Luther, banned and outlawed as he was, was not permitted to go to the diet. He stayed at Fort Coburg. From there he encouraged and comforted his friends through letters, letters which belong to the finest ever to come from his hand. He wrote to Melanchthon, whose doubts repeatedly brought him to the verge of surrendering: "You worry yourself sick because you cannot grasp how or where the matter will end. But if you could grasp it, I would have nothing whatever to do with this cause, much less

45

Leuchtenburg near Kahla

be its leader. God has put the matter in so homely a word that it does not even exist in your vocabulary or wisdom, namely, faith. That is where all things which cannot be seen or grasped have been put (Hebrews 11:1) . . . He who does not like it can lump it! If Moses had insisted on grasping how he was to escape from Pharaoh's army, Israel might still be in Egypt today. May God increase your faith and ours! If we have that, what can Satan and the whole world do to us?" On June 25, 1530, the Saxon chancelor, Christian Beyer, read the Augsburg Confession to the diet in German. It was supposed to have been read, to begin with, in Latin by the old chancelor, Dr. George Brueck. But Elector John the Steadfast succeeded in having the German version read when he declared: "In German lands the emperor might permit transactions to be carried out in German."

Renewed negotiations followed, during which Melanchthon came near the brink of retraction, but Luther reacted with vigor,

Fort Coburg

"This much is certain : as far as I am concerned, I will not budge an inch and will not agree to any changes ; I would rather be ready for the worst if they keep on this way. Let the emperor do what he can."

The diet adjourned by throwing out this challenge : The Protestants have time to reconsider until next spring ; they are to keep quiet in the meantime. The Protestant princes and free cities came together again in Smalkald to pledge to each other mutual protection and defiance. When Huldreich Zwingli was defeated by the Catholic cantons and lost his life on October 11, 1531, the South-German cities sought to join forces with Wittenberg. This was effected by the Wittenberg Concordat of 1536.

However, no collision of the hostile parties occurred as yet. Sultan Suleiman, who had besieged Vienna already in 1529, threatened both emperor and empire with a new army. The emperor's hands were now tied by this new danger, and a religious truce was concluded in Nuremberg in 1532. The emperor promised it would remain in force until a general, free council of the church could be called. The pope summoned a council which was to meet in Mantua on May 23, 1537. The Saxon elector, John Frederick, carried on lively negotiations with his allies of the Smalkald League to determine the position they should take to the pope's invitation. At the same time Luther was commissioned by the elector to set down articles of faith on which one would have to insist at the council without wavering. Luther was able to present the articles (later called the Smalkald Articles) to the court on January 3, 1537. In clear terms they bear witness to the Evangelical faith and show in what ways this differs from Catholicism. It is Luther's testament, as Chancelor Brueck expressed it. We quote just a few words : "Every child of seven among us knows, thank God, what the dear term 'church' means, namely, the holy believers and the sheep who hear their Shepherd's voice."

The Protestant estates were invited to assemble at Smalkald February 7th. The elector took with him the theologians Luther, Melanchthon, and Bugenhagen. Before the actual negotiations began, Luther became so ill that no one thought he would live. He could not void, could not hold any food in his stomach, could not sleep, and his abdomen became distended. Everything the doctors tried was of no avail. None of the drastic measures they employed had any effect. He himself thought the end was here. He made his confession to Bugenhagen and received absolution. Since he did not want to die in Smalkald, the elector had him taken, to begin with, to Tambach. The ride in the heavy wagon over the rough roads through the woods was extremely painful for Luther, yet that ride saved him. The terrific jolting relieved the condition. Now the journey to Wittenberg could be continued through Gotha, Erfurt, and Weimar. Already at Tambach he could write to his Katie : "I was dead and had commended you and the children to God and to the

St. Nicolas Church in Beuren

most gracious lords; but God did miracles on me this night, and is still doing them, because of the intercession of faithful men."

The council scheduled for Mantua never took place. The Smalkald Articles, however, are a part of Luther's precious legacy to the Christian world. For this remained his concern: to tell his beloved German people the Gospel. In the meantime the work of the Reformation continued. Luther was active as writer, church leader, organizer, preacher, and professor. A tremendous amount of work had to be accomplished. In 1534, after many repeated revisions, "the whole German Bible" appeared. Beginning in 1522, he had translated and published one book of the Bible after another. Luther's letters reveal best of all what pains he and his learned friends Bugenhagen, Melanchthon, Cruciger, and others had taken to find the right way to translate the Bible into German. He asked Spalatin on March 30, 1522: "Please let us have the names and colors of the precious stones of Revelation 21. Or will you get us the gems them-

49

selves from the court or anywhere else so that we might look at them ourselves ?" On December 12, 1522, Luther asked Spalatin for a description of a large number of beasts of prey, game animals, and creeping creatures : "In Hebrew, Latin, and Greek they are so mixed up that we have to unscramble them on the basis of the existing classes and kinds. Therefore I would like to learn to know, if possible, the name, kind, and nature of all birds of prey, all game animals, and all poisonous snakes." And in a letter to Link dated June 14, 1528, he wrote : "We are sweating and straining now to present the prophets to you in German garb. Great God, what a huge and tremendous job it is to make the Hebrew writers talk German ! They are stubborn ; they don't like to give up their Hebrew and follow the barbaric German tongue ; it is like asking a nightingale to forsake her lovely melody and imitate the cuckoo, whose monotonous call she abhors." The year 1545 brought the Latin edition of Luther's works with an important preface, which offers us an insight into his inner development.

In his personal life Luther had to endure much anguish. God blessed him with six children, but one daughter died in early infancy and another, Lenchen (Madeline), at thirteen in 1542. Before the latter's death Luther had time to send for her favorite brother Hans, who was going to school in Torgau. He arrived before the child closed her eyes forever. Standing at his child's bedside, Luther said : "I love her so very much, but, dear Lord, since it is Your will to take her, I will be pleased to know she is with You." Then he turned to her and said : "Lenchen, my little daughter, you would like to stay here with your father, but you are glad also to go to that Father, aren't you ?"—"Yes, dear father, as God wills," she answered.

The night before Lenchen died, Katie Luther had a strange dream : She saw two handsome young fellows take her daughter to her wedding. She considered the dream a good sign. When she

Marburg on the Lahn with the St. Elisabeth Church and castle

told Melanchthon about it, he was frightened and said: "The young fellows are the dear angels who will come to take this maiden into the kingdom of heaven, to the true wedding." Lenchen died that same morning.

Luther himself had to endure much sickness all his life: already quite early he suffered from gout and stones; inflammation of the middle ear, poor digestion, a leg wound, headache, and a heart condition gave him a great deal of trouble. Vexation with wavering and weak friends of the Lutheran cause, the lack of discipline among the students at Wittenberg, and many other anxieties sapped his strength.

And so his last years were filled with much bitterness. More and more he longed for a blessed end. He wrote to Amsdorf June 3, 1545: "I do not care about diets and the councils of the church, I have no faith whatever in them, expect nothing whatever from them, and feel in no way involved in them. Vanity of vanities." Then Luther recalls an injustice which had just occurred, and he writes: "Unless God intervenes, we can see this will be the spark that will ignite a huge conflagration for the punishment of Germany. But before this happens, may God take us and ours out of this valley of tribulation. No justice, no one ruling the empire—an empire without government—the empire's dregs and last drop!" This bitterness accounted for his decision in 1545 to leave Wittenberg for good. He had accompanied Cruciger to an arbitration meeting in Zeitz. It was meant to be a pleasure trip for him. From Zeitz he wrote his wife he had no intention of returning. "Anything to leave and get out of that Sodom! . . . Day after tomorrow I will go to Merseburg. For Prince George has urgently requested it. Would rather turn back and beg before torturing myself and upsetting my poor, old last days with that confused mess in Wittenberg and with the loss of my hard, precious work." However, Luther did not abide by his resolution. When various delegates from the city of Wittenberg, also from the university and the elector, came to him, he let them talk him out of it. He did it the more readily when he was given the assurance that the deplorable state of moral affairs in Wittenberg was to be remedied. And this did not remain only a promise on his part. It is true he took his time in returning: he first consecrated Prince George of Anhalt as the episcopal administrator in Merseburg, he preached in Halle—but he did return. On November 10, 1545, he was able to celebrate his birthday for the last time among his old friends. Melanchthon, Bugenhagen, Cruciger, Major, Paul Eber, and several others were present. Premonitions of death filled his heart.

A week later he concluded the exposition of Genesis with the words: "There, that's the good book of Genesis; may our Lord God grant that it be done better after me! I cannot keep on any

The Wartburg
in the 14th century

View toward Eisenach

Meiningen, view toward the apse of the city church

longer, I am weak; ask God to grant me a gracious and blessed final hour."

When one considers how this man had to contend with pressures from without, ill health, and the spiritual onslaughts of the old evil Foe, the profusion of work he accomplished is beyond comprehension.

His literary works and correspondence alone could have occupied a whole life span. And how often he preached, all the more when he had to substitute for the city pastor Bugenhagen (Dr. Pomeranus), while the latter was carrying out the work of the Reformation in the cities of North Germany! How many people called on him to seek his counsel and aid! In him all felt the dynamic strength of faith. This strength alone made him capable of his great work and helped him to withstand the inner struggles and all the outer pressures.

His death came as a surprise to everybody. He was staying with his three sons in Eisleben, where he had come to settle a dispute among the counts of Mansfeld. He succeeded in reconciling the parties. Luther was still able to preach four sermons in Eisleben. He had to cut the fourth sermon short because he felt weak. February 17 he complained of feeling pressure on his chest. Around 11 o'clock in the evening he fell asleep. During the night, at one, he called his servant Ambrose and Doctor Jonas. "O Lord God! Doctor Jonas, I am so sick, there is such a heavy pressure on my chest. Oh, I shall stay in Eisleben." Then he went back to his room and started to pray: "My heavenly Father! Eternal, merciful God! You have revealed Your dear Son, our Lord Jesus Christ, to me; I have taught and confessed Him; I love Him and honor Him as my Savior and Redeemer, Him whom the godless persecute, dishonor, and slander. Take my poor soul to be with You."

Then he prayed three times: "Into Your hands I commend my spirit. You have redeemed me, O God of truth. Yes, God so loved the world." The end appeared near. Only a distinct "Yes" came from his lips yet as Doctor Jonas and Michael Coelius shouted into his ear: "Dearest Father, after all you believe in Christ, your Savior and Redeemer." After that his brow and face became cold.

His rich life came to a close on February 18, 1546, in the city in which he had been born. His body was taken to Wittenberg through Halle. There, as he was brought into the Market Church, which was dimly lit by candles but filled to the last seat, the people received him with his wonderful hymn: "From Depths of Woe I Cry to You." The chronicler says that they "with plaintive voice wept the Psalm rather than sang it."

He was laid to rest in the Castle Church of Wittenberg.

At his grave Melanchthon said: "We are now just like poor, forsaken orphans, who have had such an excellent man for a father and are now robbed of him. Since we need to obey God and submit to His will, we will always remember our dear father and let nothing tear him out of our hearts. For his sake we should thank God and rejoice with him in that blessed, eternal fellowship which he now has with God and His Son, our Lord Jesus Christ, and with the blessed fathers and prophets and apostles, a fellowship for which he constantly and trustfully longed and waited in his life." However, what Luther wrote in his explanations of the 95 Theses is his legacy to us :

My dear Redeemer and Savior, my Lord Jesus Christ, is enough for me, I will sing to Him as long as I live.

To be a Christian and not have Christ is impossible ;
but he who has Christ also has all that Christ Himself is.

	1455 John Gutenberg prints the 42-line Bible
	1460 Tilman Riemenschneider born
	1466 Mentel prints the first German Bible in Strasbourg
	1471 Albrecht Duerer born
	1472 Numbering the pages of a book with Arabic numerals introduced
	1475 Michelangelo born
1483, Nov. 10, Martin Luther born in Eisleben	
1484, May, the Luther family moves to Mansfeld	
	1485 Ulrich Zwingli born Construction of the walls and towers of the Kremlin begun
	1492 Columbus discovers America
	1493 Hartmann Schedel composes his chronicle of the world
	1494 Hans Sachs born
1497 —1498 School days in Magdeburg	1497 Leipzig Fair licensed by the emperor Philip Melanchthon born
1498 —1501 Martin Luther attends the Latin School in Eisenach	
	1499 Switzerland becomes independent after its secession from the German Empire
1501 —1505, April, Luther a student at Erfurt in the college of liberal arts	1501 Albrecht Duerer, woodcut series, "The Great Passion"

1502 Founding of Wittenberg University
Peasant revolt at Bruchsal (Baden) led by Fritz Joss (The Bundschuh Union) fails

1503 Pope gives the Teutonic Knights permission to sell indulgences

1504 Tetzel begins the indulgence traffic

1505, Jan. 7, Luther receives his M.A.
July 17, Luther enters the Augustinian Order at Erfurt

1506 Construction of St. Peter's at Rome begins

1507, May, ordination to the priesthood in the cathedral at Erfurt

1508 Luther moves into the Augustinian cloister in Wittenberg; lectures there at the university founded in 1502

1509, October, Luther returns to Erfurt

1510, November, the Augustinian Order sends Luther to Rome

1511, April, Luther returns to Erfurt and moves to Wittenberg

1512 Doctor of Theology, Professor of Holy Scripture, Luther goes to Cologne to attend a chapter of his order
Matthias Gruenewald completes the Isenheimer altar-piece
Michelangelo completes painting the ceiling of the Sistine Chapel
Leo X becomes pope
The archbishop of Mainz pledges the indulgence proceeds to the pope

1513 Lectures on the Psalms begin

58

1515 Lectures on the Epistle to the Romans	"Letters of Obscure Men" against church and state
1516 Lectures on the Epistle to the Galatians	Greek edition of New Testament by Erasmus of Rotterdam
	Thomas More outlines the communistic ideal state of "Utopia"
	Failure of the peasant revolt of the Bundschuh Union
1517, Oct. 31, 95 Theses posted on the door of the Castle Church in Wittenberg	
1518, April, Heidelberg Disputation	Melanchthon's Greek grammar
August, summons to Rome	Raphael paints the Sistine Madonna
Oct. 12 —14, Luther's defense before Cardinal Cajetan in Augsburg	
1519, Jan. 15, conference between Luther and the chamberlain von Miltitz in Altenburg	Death of Leonardo da Vinci
	Death of Maximilian I; Charles V becomes German emperor
July 4 —14, Leipzig disputation with Dr. Eck and Carlstadt	
1520, December, papal bull threatening excommunication burned in Wittenberg	Florian Geyer demands abolition of estate privileges
1521, Jan. 3, Bull *Decet Romanum Pontificium* excommunicating Luther goes into effect	Ulrich von Hutten's "Conversation Booklet" appears
April 2 —26, Luther travels to the Diet of Worms	
May 4, Luther is "kidnapped" and taken to the Wartburg	
May 26, Luther put under the imperial ban	Death of Pope Leo X
December, Luther, begins to translate the New Testament	
December 2 —11, Luther's secret journey to Wittenberg	

59

1522, March 6, return to Wittenberg from the Wartburg	First circumnavigation of the world
1523, Pentecost, "Concerning the Order of the Church Service in the Congregation"	Death of Sickingen Hans Sachs' Luther song, "The Wittenberg Nightingale" Death of Ulrich von Hutten
1524 Publication of "The Spiritual Songbook" (32 hymns, 24 by Luther) "A Charge to the Councilors of All Cities in the German Nation to Erect and Maintain Christian Schools" Luther discards the monk's cowl—introduces the black gown as the dress for clergy	Peasant War begins
1525 Writings pertaining to the Peasants' War Marriage to Katherine von Bora	Execution of Thomas Muentzer Death of Frederick the Wise
1526, June, Luther's first child, Hans, born Recognition of Protestantism by the Diet of Speyer	Hans Holbein Jr. completes the woodcut series "Dance of Death"
1527, summer, Martin Luther becomes gravely ill	Founding of the Protestant University of Marburg 1528, April 6, death of Albrecht Duerer Copernicus defends his heliocentric theory of the universe Death of Tilman Riemenschneider
1529, April, protest of the Protestant estates at the Diet of Speyer The Small Catechism October, theological discussion in Marburg (Luther, Zwingli, Melanchthon, Jonas, Bucer)	

1529 *A Mighty Fortress Is Our God*

1530 Diet of Augsburg
Luther at Fort Coburg
Death of Luther's father

Charles V is crowned German
emperor by the pope
Formation of the Smalkald League

1531 Death of Luther's mother

Death of Zwingli

1534 First complete edition of
Luther's Bible translation

Frenchman Jacques Cartier
discovers Canada
1535 Olivetanus translates the
Bible into French

1536 Smalkald Articles

1537, February, "Diet of the
Princes" at Smalkald

Reformation in Norway

1540, June 28, Luther comforts sick
Melanchthon in Weimar
July 20 — 24, Luther, Melanchthon, and Justus Jonas confer
at Eisenach regarding the
marriage of Landgrave
Philip of Hesse

1541 *Against Hanns Worst*

1542 Luther makes his will
Negotiations with Landgrave
Philip of Hesse and Elector
John Frederick
Last Lecture on Genesis

1543 *The Jews and their Lies*

Death of Hans Holbein Jr.
Death of Copernicus

1545 *Against the Papacy at Rome,
Founded by the Devil*
Luther declines to take part
in the Council of Trent

1546, Feb. 18, Luther's death

Outbreak of the Smalkald War

INDEX OF PERSONS

INDEX OF PLACES

You shall find strength

in quietness and hope

Isaiah 30:15

Luther's motto

Ancestral home in Moehra

Luther's father belonged to the Luder clan, a widely represented Thuringian peasant family, whose ancestral home in Moehra, north of Salzungen, is still known today. On the way back from the Diet at Worms (1521) Luther visited his relatives living there. A linden tree under which he preached then calls attention to this event. Of course, it is no longer the original tree; that was destroyed by a storm about 130 years ago. Also the house was replaced, already in 1618, by a new structure on the same site.

Luther's father, Hans Luder

Luther's father, Hans Luder—it was only Martin Luther who later changed the name to Luther—was an extremely diligent and ambitious man. As it was the custom for the youngest son to inherit the estate of his father, he decided to be a miner. Is it any wonder that he wanted to "have his son be something" and would not grant him permission to enter the monastery?

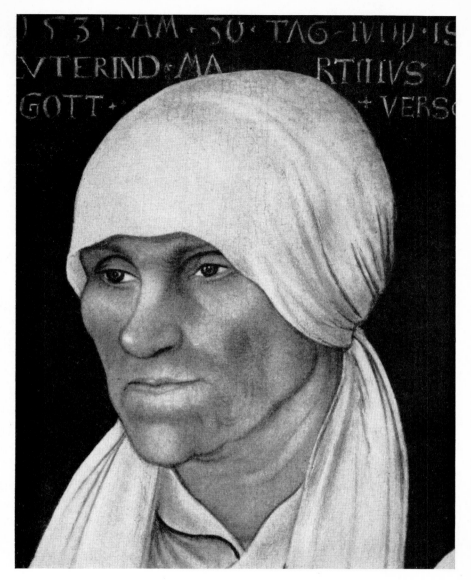

Luther's mother, Margaret Luder

Luther's mother, Margaret Luder, b. Ziegler (also Lindemann), worked just as hard and was just as concerned about the family as her husband. Because they were never too well off, she could not devote all her time to bringing up the large family they had but had to help out wherever she was needed.

My parents were poor at first. My father was a poor miner. The firewood needed to keep her children warm my mother carried home on her back. Hard work was their lot. Today nobody in the world would put up with it.

One should not punish children too hard : my father once whipped me so severely that I began avoiding him ; he yearned for me to come back to him, until he got me used to him again. So I do not like to whip my little Hans too much. He might become timid and hate me ; I could think of no greater grief than that. This is how God does it : My children, I am going to chastise you, but through someone else : the devil or the world. But then, if you will cry and run to Me, I will rescue you and comfort you again. For our Lord God would not want us to hate Him.

The house in Eisleben where Luther was born (view from the backyard)

November 10, 1483, Luther was born in Eisleben and was baptized Martin the following day in St. Peter's Church.

Eisleben, copper engraving from Merian's Topography of 1650

Merian's city views give us an impression of German cities in the Middle Ages. On them the "face" of every city is retained to a certain extent. These reproductions have been chosen to take us into every city which was intimately connected with Luther's life and the Reformation. Martin Luther's life and career begin in Eisleben, they end in Eisleben—however, in between lies the beginning of a new epoch.

72

My parents were so strict with me that I became timid through it. My mother once whipped me for the sake of a miserable nut until I bled ; their severity and the strict life we led together were behind my running into a monastery and becoming a monk later on. They meant extremely well but could not distinguish the dispositions and punish accordingly. For when we punish, the rod must have an apple next to it.

Mansfeld around the year 1650

Within the walls of this small mining town Martin Luther spent his childhood and received his first schooling in the town school.—Mansfeld Castle, familiar to many of us, still stands high above the town.

Right: Mansfeld Castle, a detail from the illustration on page 74

74

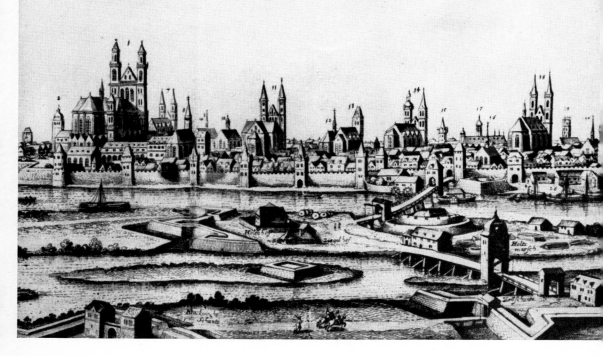

Magdeburg around the year 1650

Magdeburg has not only an accidental significance for the Reformation because Luther's parents sent him to school there; it was among the first German cities that fully embraced Protestantism and has been called with good reason "our Lord's Secretariat."

76

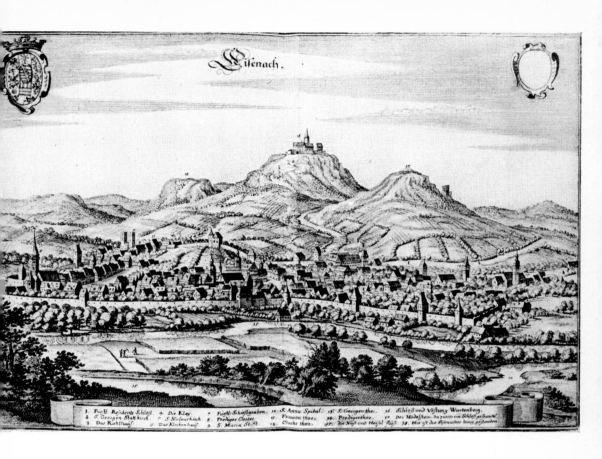

Eisenach around the year 1650

Did the young student Martin Luther ever dream, when looking up at the Wartburg, what significance it would have for him one day?

Statues of Luther and Bach
in Eisenach

Eisenach is known
in all Protestant
countries not only
as the city of Luther
but also as the birthplace of
John Sebastian Bach ;
because of his oratorios
and cantatas the latter
was called
"the fifth Evangelist."

The Luther House in Eisenach in its present state

In this house of the Schalbe-Cotta family Martin Luther probably received his first deeper religious impressions; these went far beyond the religious instruction received in school and decisively influenced his later life.

Right: Lantern on the Luther House

This lantern bears witness to the quality of German craftmanship; we are glad it is still hanging there on the Luther House.

You parents can leave your children no better or safer treasure than to let them study and learn the liberal arts ; house and home may disappear, but education you can take with you and it will endure.

Some schoolmasters are as cruel as hangmen. I was once whipped fifteen times in one morning without deserving it. I was supposed to decline and conjugate and had not learned it.

A school should make children sensible people who promote the welfare of the community and state.

Music is a precious, glorious gift of God and close to theology. I would not trade what little music I know for something more impressive. Young people should constantly be exposed to it, for it produces fine, adept people . . .

Music is the greatest gift of God. It is a great antidote to Satan, for it drives away many severe temptations. The devil simply cannot stand it.

Front door of Luther's secondary school in Eisenach

It was not only Martin Luther who received his final schooling at St. George's parish school before attending the university ; also John Sebastian Bach went through this door every day when he was a student here two hundred years later.

I am sure it is no secret to any Christian that it is a good thing and pleases God to sing spiritual songs. The prophets and kings in the Old Testament are an example to everyone ; they praised God by singing and making up songs to the accompaniment of cymbals and stringed instruments ; but beyond that, this custom, and especially Psalm singing, has been known to the whole Christian church from the beginning. Yes, even St. Paul authorizes it in 1 Corinthians 14.

Singing is the finest art and exercise . . . singers are not sad, but on the contrary they drive out all cares from the mind.

Once when some singers were guests of Luther, he said as they sang beautiful, lovely motets : "Since the Lord our God has poured such noble gifts into this life, what is it going to be like in yonder eternal life where everything will be so completely perfect and gay ?"

Martin Luther as a street singer before Mrs. Cotta

Historical painters from the nineteenth century were fond of using Luther's life as subject matter.—In spite of its artistic and historical imperfection this painting gives us a vivid impression from the life of young Luther.

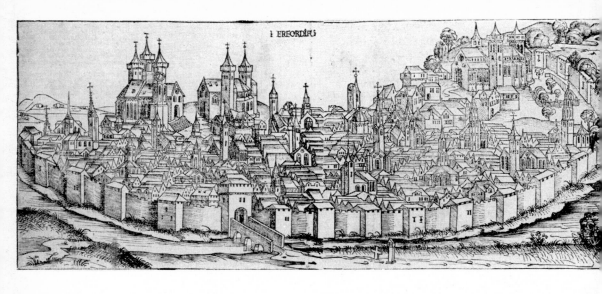

Erfurt at Luther's time
According to a woodcut from Hartmann Schedel's "World Chronicle" of 1493

This woodcut offers us a typical view of the layout of Erfurt at Luther's time.
The many small parish and cloister churches are overshadowed by the cathedral
and the St. Severus Church—symbols of the intense piety of this age.

Right: Cathedral and St. Severus Church
Detail from the illustration on page 86

86

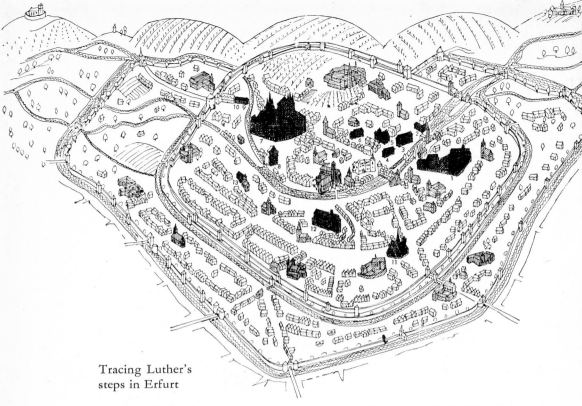

Tracing Luther's steps in Erfurt

1. Augustinian monastery; admission on July 17, 1505; novice and monk till October 1508 and from October 1509 till 1511; sermon on April 7, 1521, while going to Worms.
2. St. George's College at Lehmann Bridge; Luther here as a student 1501(2) to 1505.
3. Great College; main building of the philosophical faculty; registration; frequented disputations and library.
4. Amplonius College at Porta Coeli; where Luther first lived as student? Repeated visits.
5. St. Michael's Church, the chapel of the philosophical faculty; sermon on October 21, 1522.
6. Engelsburg, Allerheiligen Street; humanist center; residence of the physician Dr. Sturz, who was on friendly terms with Luther; rest stop for Luther during his illness of March 4 and 5, 1537, while returning from Smalkald.
7. Cathedral and Auditorium Coelicum; ordination to priesthood 1507; attended lectures in theology 1509—10.
8. Tall Lily, private beer garden, later an inn; allegedly imprisoned here March 2, 1522, while returning from the Wartburg to Wittenberg.
9. School of Law, Mainzerhof Street; attended law lectures.
10. St. Mary's College; meeting with his former professor Jodocus Trutvetter May 9, 1518, while returning from a convention of his order in Heidelberg.
11. Merchants' Church; sermons October 22, 1522.
12. Barefoot Friars Church; sermon on October 11, 1529, while returning from the Marburg theological debate.
13. Schlehendorn Inn; last stay in Erfurt July 4, 5, and 27, 1540, when going to Eisenach and when returning to Wittenberg.

Right: The old university, destroyed in World War II, and St. Michael's Church

Luther related that, on the road near Stotternheim not far from Erfurt, he had become so panic-stricken that he had cried out in terror: "Saint Anne, help, I promise to become a monk!" Afterwards I regretted the vow. Many advised me not to keep it, but I insisted on keeping it. On the following day I invited some of my good friends to a farewell party so they might be on hand the next day to see me off to the monastery. But when they hesitated, I said: "Today you are seeing me for the last time." Then they accompanied me, with tears in their eyes. My father was quite exasperated over my vow, but I adhered firmly to my resolution and never thought of leaving the monastery again.

I left parents and relatives and, opposed by all, put on a monk's cowl and ran into the monastery because I was convinced I would be obeying God in a noble manner with such a way of life and those menial tasks.

God placed His church in the midst of the world, among countless trades and callings, not that Christians might become monks but that we might live sociably and in fellowship, giving evidence of our works and exercising our faith among men.

Right: University register with Martin Luther's name

Because the reputation of Erfurt University eclipsed the fame of other German universities, Luther's father chose to have his son study at the more distant alma mater in Erfurt rather than at the University of Leipzig, which was nearer.

¶ Totum

Conradus Kareman de Halberstadt.
Henricus gran de brunswigk.
Ioannes mechtildt de regio stagno.
Henricus stüper de lüneburgk.
Georius westhede lubicensis.
Ioannes tindalm hamburgensis.
Michael hoffman de kesten.
Ioannes bockel de minselt.
Wolffgangus galt de wendingen.
Balthasir sculten de breydenstein.
Ioannes Larve de embegke.
Henricus schwartz de temyten.
Georius leynaghel de salyburga.
Paulus werner de markelßheym.
Ioannes Rymbach de Aw.
Ioannes holingher de weygterstevm.
Ludewicus christiam de tratteborgk.
Ioannes hüen de frangkenbergk.
Petrus Strecher de werpach.
Nicolaus carpentary de magstedt.
Ioannes de Sthawenbergk nobilis.
Theodericus tremer de lobenstem.
Ioannes taltenbergk de Salya
Ioannes de laurencien de ynigtaiua
Petrus boxstar de langen.
Ioannes behe de assindia.
Henricus preyn de lemego
Ioannes Schynthel de komgelehe.
Ioannes bengkman de kirchhagen.
Nicolaus Grimer de franken
hulen
Laurencius Trürber de slmen.
Ioannes penderhans de Syeghen.

Andreas Schönenbergde elbingk.
Lubericus Schürer de lympurgk.
Erhardus hoch de wydha.
Hermannus nydernhofer de marp
purgk.
Antonius Currikicis de allen
dorf an der Lümbe.
+ Martinus ludher ex manßfelt
Ioannes Sthaffuecht de allendorff.
Sigismundus kirchener de Monster.
Iohannes orthusm de drebus
Iodocius barbitonsoris de Speyern.
Iacobus bilich de Aqvil.
Sebastianus flebergk de
Theodericus Geymmelli   Sula
Wolffgangus setrilstedr de Schlusingk
Melchiar fröwel de tanewerffen
Ioannes kevkys Erphordiensis.
Appollinaris pfhliger de kömgehofen.
Bernhardus fabri de karlleborgk
Frater Lüdewicus fabri de Cassel ex
dms Carmelitarim,

Ioannes   garlop de lüneburgk
Gotfridus germani.
Valentinus
               de pock germani no
Otto   biles.
Hartmannis müris de Gromgen.
Eustachius toler de kaufbeuren.
Matthias friderici de Isleuben.
Ioannes beyl de Hanaw.
Ioannes bez de franckfordia.
Colnius olburgk de witlich.
Conradus wecheman de oimghen.
Wendelmus Geiringher de bietica.
Henricus Trammm de Ilsnach.

The Augustinian monastery from the south

Of the five monasteries in the city of Erfurt Luther chose the so-called "Black Monastery", the convent of the Augustinian Eremites. In this monastic community, the goal of which was total asceticism, he wanted to dedicate himself completely to God.

Model of the Erfurt Augustinian monastery used in its restoration in the years
1936—1938

This picture shows us the complete layout of a monastery typical of many monasteries of the Middle Ages.

Interior view of the Augustinian church in its present state

It was in the monastery church that Martin Luther made his profession, that is, took the three vows of obedience, poverty, and chastity. By this step he was definitely received into the order.

The slab on the tomb of Father and Professor Zacharias, d. 1428

On this slab Luther lay with arms outstretched in the form of a cross (as prescribed by the regulations) as he was accepted into the monastery. It is the memorial slab of Professor of Theology John Zacharias, who convicted Huss of heresy in a disputation at the Council of Constance and so brought about his condemnation.

Luther's cell in the monastery. Before the fire of 1872

In the loneliness of his monastery cell Luther strove to attain God's grace with prayer and ascetic exercises far exceeding all prescribed regulations of the monastery.

Monastery garden, view from Luther's cell

98

The cloister of the orphanage

In the year 1669 the monastery was rebuilt into a Protestant orphanage. Our picture shows the building toward the end of the 17th century.

Left: Cloister

"Silence" was one of the cardinal laws of the monastery. This cloister breathes meditative stillness; its beauty and its inviting peace captivate us even today.

Chapter Hall of the Augustinian church
From the first half of the 14th century

The "chapter hall" takes its name from the daily reading of a chapter from the
Bible. It served the monks as a common meditation and assembly room.

Guest House of the Augustinian monastery

Our present-day youth hostel certainly has for its forerunners the guest houses of the monasteries, in which every passerby found welcome lodging.

View from the St. John's tower toward the Augustinian church
In the background, the cathedral and St. Severus Church

The ideal of monastic poverty is revealed in the simple church steeple which dispenses with all ornamental accessories.

Right: View of the old city of Erfurt toward St. Mary's Cathedral and St. Severus Church

Rome in the 16th century

As a monk I tried very hard and took the greatest pains to live as the rules prescribed. I would always first repent of all my sins and then confess and enumerate them ; often I even repeated the confession, and then I would diligently perform the penance imposed on me. And still my conscience could never achieve security. I had constant doubts about the sufficiency of my efforts, saying to myself : You did not do this right, weren't contrite enough, omitted that from confession, etc. And so, the longer I tried to heal my weak and troubled conscience by following human rules, the more uncertain, weak, and confused it became each day.

Illustration on pages 104 and 105 : Rome in the 16th century. Luther may have found the "Eternal City" looking just about like the view represented by Donato Bertelli in his engraving. In the winter of 1510—11 he traveled to Rome on foot in the service of the Augustinian Eremites of Erfurt, to serve as travel companion to an older priest from Erfurt. During his 4-week stay he also visited the famous sites as a pilgrim.—To be sure, this print of the Italian engraver does not pretend to be topographically accurate ; its realistic elements are mixed here, as in so many city views of that time, with elements of fantasy.

Right : St. Martin's Day in Erfurt

Every year thousands of children and adults meet on the eve of Luther's birthday to honor the great Reformer with a festive parade of Chinese lanterns.

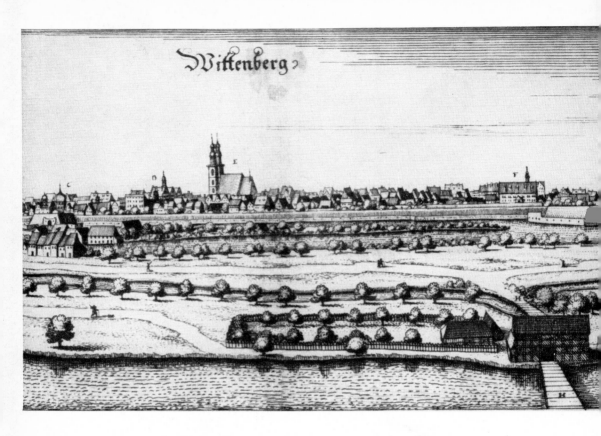

Wittenberg, according to an engraving from Merian's Topography of 1650

At Luther's time Wittenberg was only a small and historically unimportant town; it had no special advantage or distinction over other towns. With its 2,000 inhabitants it might easily have given the impression of being a small rural market town rather than the seat of a university.

Right: The Luther House in the 18th century

Since his first stay in Wittenberg Luther lived in the monastery of the Augustinian Eremites. After the dissolution of the monastery in consequence of the Reformation, Elector Frederick the Wise gave this house to Luther in 1525. Luther and his family occupied the right wing; in the left wing, both in the large and the small classroom, he gave his lectures.

The collegiate Castle Church of All Saints in Wittenberg

Even individual churches received authorization from the pope to show their relics to the faithful one day a year and to grant them partial or full indulgence for money on this occasion. The Castle Church in Wittenberg also had acquired this permission and on All Saints' Day (November 1) attracted innumerable people with its more than 5,000 relics.

Left: The Luther House in its present state

The rooms of the Luther House now house the Reformation-history collections of the Luther Hall museum.

III

Market Place in Wittenberg. Today Luther's city, Wittenberg, is the center of attraction for many visitors from all Protestant countries in the world.

Left : View from the tower of the City Church toward the Castle Church

Well in the Luther courtyard

The Frederickana in Wittenberg—
the old university buildings on College Street

In 1502 Elector Frederick the Wise founded the university in Wittenberg. Six years later Luther's order sent the young priest to Wittenberg. Here he was expected to complete his study of theology and give lectures in the liberal arts.

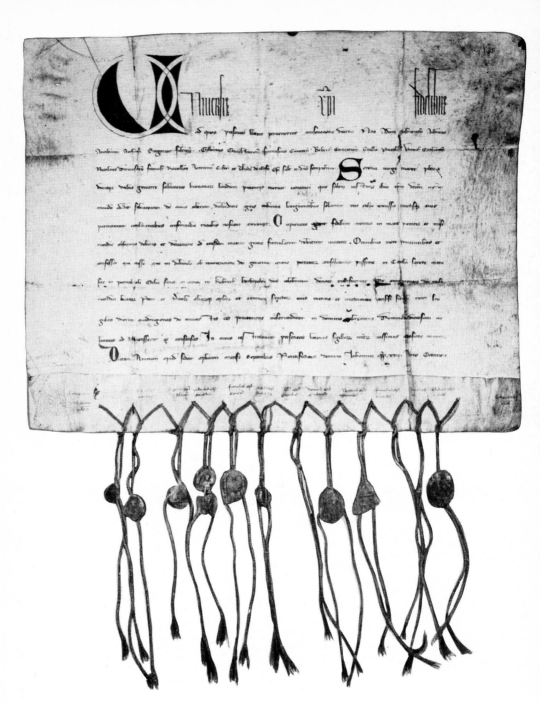

Innomine domini nostri iesu christi amen. Pateat vniuersis quo p
pussione sieda z theueru
qui iam oras Jtalie preoccupauit. ordinata per sanctissimu dominu nostru Sirtu diuina prouidentia
papa quartu Laurentius · · · · De Marcellis
statuta p cude dnm papa fec · z tributione. Et ppterea auctoritate prefati dni pape ipse idulgentia
habet plenissima omniu suoz peccatoz z potestate eligedi tibi confessore idoneu etia cuiuscuq religi-
onis. qui audita etus confessione possit z debeat eu absoluere ab omnibus peccatis z excomunica-
tionibus a iure uel per statuta quecunq promulgatis z sedi apostolice reseruatis qtumcunq enormi-
bus semel in uita. duintararat. de non reseruatis sedi apostolice totiens quotiens id petierit. Et in mortis
articulo plenariam omnium peccatorum suorum impendere remissionem. non obstantibus quibuscu-
q reseruationibus a prefato pontifice aut eius predecessoribus factis ut i bullis eiusde datio. ano dni
1480. pridie nonas decembris plenius continet. In cui rei side ego Fr ····· de ···· ordis
deputat sup hoc negotio a reuerēdo patre fratre angelo de clauasio ordinis mioz de obseruatia uica-
rio generali z comissario apostolico super pdictis bullis exequedis. hanc scripturam fieri fec z sigillo
muniui. ··· Die · Mensis ····· 1481.

Indulgence letter from Brandenburg

One of the indulgence blanks used by Tetzel. On the prepared forms only the
buyer's name and the date still needed to be written in. Forgiveness of sin could
be bought for money in this way.

Left: Authorization for dispensing indulgences

The authorization for dispensing indulgences was given by the pope or local
cardinals for a certain territory; the authorization was written on parchment and
appended with seals.—The illustration here is of an original now in the possession of Luther Hall.

118

Section of the "theses door"

Luther's fifth thesis reads: "The pope will not and cannot remit any punishment except what he has imposed of his own will or according to papal statutes."
—In this thesis Luther denies indulgences the power to remit any punishment except the temporal penances imposed by the church; the punishments ordained by God are not lifted by an indulgence.

Left: The "theses door" of the Castle Church at Wittenberg
In 1858 a new door was cast in bronze to replace the old wooden door destroyed by fire.

Driven by a very deep sense of pastoral responsibility, Luther had condemned the indulgence traffic in sermons as early as October 31, 1516, and February 1517. Since these attempts to call for a reconsideration of penance failed, Luther decided to invite a public debate. On the evening of October 31, 1517, he nailed his 95 Theses on the door of the Castle Church in Wittenberg.

I have learned from my own experience and that of others how peaceable and quiet the devil can be in the first year of monastic life.

I, too, wanted to be a holy, devout monk and prepared myself religiously for mass and prayer. But even when I was in my most devout state of mind, I went to the altar as a doubter, and as a doubter I left it again. When I had said my penance, I still doubted ; when I had not said it, I was in despair. For we were completely under the delusion that, unless we were perfectly pure and free from sin like the saints in heaven, we could not pray and would not be heard, and that it would be much better to quit praying altogether in such a case.

In the monastery I was holier than I am now—according to outward appearance. I prayed, kept more vigils, was continent, tortured my flesh, in short, my whole life was splendid in the eyes of everyone but mine, for my heart was torn and troubled.

Martin Luther as monk. Engraving by Luke Cranach, Sr., 1520

The year 1520 was the crucial year of the Reformation. Martin Luther carried
on the work with the courage of faith ; beside other things, this year saw the
three revolutionary documents : "An Address to the Christian Nobility of the
German Nation Concerning the Reform of Christendom," "The Babylonian
Captivity of the Church," and "Christian Liberty." Luther's inner tension and
his determination born of faith have been preserved by Cranach in this engraving ; underneath he put the words : "Luther himself engraved the eternal image
of his spirit, Luke's stylus only his mortal facial features."

Bulla contra errores
Martini Lutheri
& sequacium.

122

Burning of the
papal bull
which threatened
Luther with
excommunication

In the year 1520 a papal bull threatened Luther with excommunication. It condemned 41 of Luther's statements as heresy, demanded that all his writings be burned, and ordered him to recant. On December 10, 1520, after his writings had been burned in Louvain (Belgium), Luther, surrounded by many students, threw the papal bull into a bonfire in front of the east gate of Wittenberg. Our illustration reproduces a representation from the 19th century.

Left: Title page of the excommunication bull

The papal bull which was meant to exclude Luther from the church and to outlaw him was practically ineffectual in Germany.

I, Doctor Martin, was called and compelled to become a doctor of theology out of sheer obedience, without my thanks (whether I wanted to or not). So I had to accept the doctoral [teaching] office and swear and promise to teach and preach my precious Scriptures unalloyed and with faithfulness.

Staupitz called me to Wittenberg and ordered me to lecture and to preach, and gave orders that all lessons stop at mealtime and the Bible be read. And while I lectured and preached here, I always stayed with the Scriptures. That is why I was known here as a heretic for two whole years.

Martin Luther with doctor's hood. Engraving by Luke Cranach, Sr., 1521

In 1521 Charles V convoked the Diet at Worms. The doctor of theology Martin Luther was determined to risk everything for his faith. His journey to Worms resembled a triumphal march. In Erfurt the city council welcomed him in front of the city gates, and he had to preach in the overcrowded church of the Augustinian monastery.

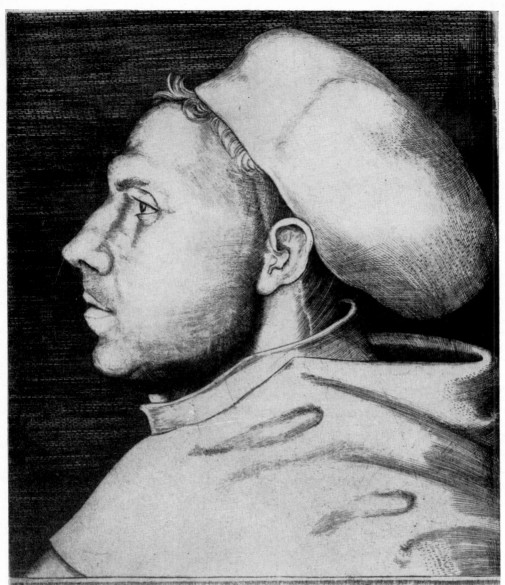

LVCAE · OPVS · EFFIGIES · HAEC · EST · MORITVRA · LVTHERI ·
AETHERNAM · MENTIS · EXPRIMIT · IPSE · SVAE ·
M · D · X · X · I ·

125

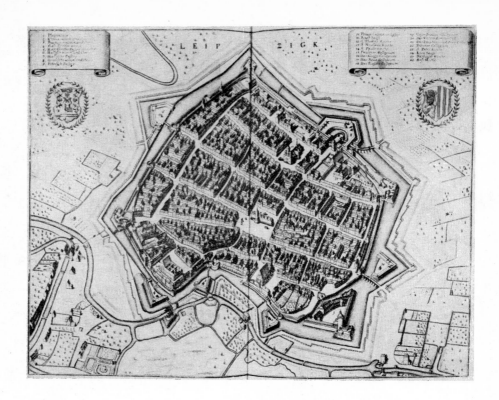

City map of Leipzig from the year 1650

At the request of Duke George the Bearded of Saxony a theological disputation between Luther and Eck was held in July 1519 in the Pleissenburg at Leipzig. Since the meeting led to no agreement, Duke George became Luther's bitter opponent. His resolute stand here, however, gained Luther the friendship of the humanist Melanchthon.

Right: John Huss, 1369—1415

John Huss, a professor at Prague, was one of the forerunners of the Reformation. His vehement opposition as university professor and preacher to the abuses within the Catholic Church brought him a large following. In an attempt to bring about a settlement of the differences of opinion, the pope ordered Huss to appear at the Council of Constance (1414), under the assurance of safe-conduct. The council condemned his teachings as heresy and, since he was not willing to recant, sentenced him to be burned at the stake.

A mighty Fortress is our God,
A trusty Shield and Weapon ;
He helps us free from ev'ry need
That hath us now o'ertaken.
The old evil Foe
Now means deadly woe ;
Deep guile and great might
Are his dread arms in fight ;
On earth is not his equal.

With might of ours can naught be done,
Soon were our loss effected ;
But for us fights the Valiant One,
Whom God Himself elected.
Ask ye, Who is this ?
Jesus Christ it is,
Of Sabaoth Lord,
And there's none other God ;
He holds the field forever.

Though devils all the world should fill,
All eager to devour us,
We tremble not, we fear no ill,
They shall not overpower us.
This world's prince may still
Scowl fierce as he will,
He can harm us none,
He's judged ; the deed is done ;
One little word can fell him.

The Word they still shall let remain
Nor any thanks have for it ;
He's by our side upon the plain
With His good gifts and Spirit.
And take they our life,
Goods, fame, child, and wife,
Let these all be gone,
They yet have nothing won ;
The kingdom ours remaineth.

Leipzig Disputation between Luther and Eck

Luther remained convinced that it is not necessary to recognize the pope in order to be saved. Yes, even councils can err as is evident from the conviction of Huss by the Council of Constance.—Our illustration shows a representation from the 19th century.

Left: Martin Luther, A Mighty Fortress Is Our God, 1529

If someone attacks your position and says : "We need an interpretation by the church fathers, Scripture is obscure," you should say : That is not true. There is no book in the whole world that is clearer than Holy Scripture ; in comparison with other books it is like the sun compared with other lights. They say such things only to lead us away from Scripture and set themselves up as our masters, so that we might believe their fantastic claims.

It is a great and horrible insult to all Christendom and a blasphemy against Holy Scripture to say that Holy Scripture is obscure and not clear enough for everyone to understand it, learn from it to believe, and show his faith. – You may be sure of it and need have no doubts : there is nothing brighter than the sun, that is, Scripture ; even if a cloud passes in front of the sun, it is still the same bright sun. And so, if you find an obscure passage in Scripture, do not despair ; you may be sure the same truth in back of it is clearly expressed in another place ; let him who cannot understand what is obscure stay with what is clear.

To the Christians at Wittenberg; written from the Wartburg prior to August 12, 1521.

The printed title page of a sermon Luther preached in Leipzig

How rapidly Luther's sermons spread is revealed by this printing done in 1519, the year of the disputation. The woodcut is one of the oldest representations of Luther, the inscription is printed in reverse and reads : "Doctor Martin Luther—Augustinian—Wittenberg."

Ein Sermon geprediget tzu Leipßgk vff in Schloß am tag Petri vñ pau-

li ym.xviiij. Jar / durch den wirdigen vater Doctorem
Martinũ Luther augustiner zu Wittenburgk / mit
entschuldigung etzlicher artickel / ßo ym von
etzlichen seiner abgünstigen zugemessen
seyn / In der zeit der Disputacion zu
Leipßgk gehalten.

⁋ Gedruckt zu Leypßgk durch Wolffgang Stöckel im Jar.1519.

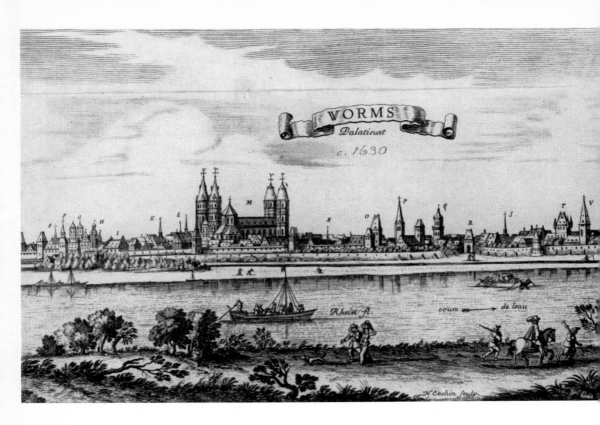

Worms, engraving from Merian's Topography

Behind the wide river Rhine we see the skyline of Worms, dotted with towers and standing out boldly against the sky. It is here that Luther came in April 1521 to appear before the emperor and the historic session of the diet of the realm to defend with unshakable faith in God his conviction that only the word of Holy Scripture should carry weight with a Christian.

Right : The cathedral in Worms ; steel engraving around 1840

The large, bold architecture of the Romanesque cathedral, consecrated in 1181, towers above the snug bustle of the narrow city streets below. When Luther tried to get into the meeting of the diet in the episcopal palace on April 18, 1521, the streets were so jammed with his enthusiastic supporters that he got through only with an escort and in a roundabout way.

132

133

Martin Luther, portrait by Luke Cranach, Jr.

Luke Cranach, Jr., like his father before him, was also an ardent supporter of
Luther's doctrine. He painted this likeness of the Reformer in 1579—hence
after his death—and honored him by inscribing it: "... a prophet of God,
under whose leadership faith was brought to light again ..."

At Worms I stood firm before the emperor and the whole empire, evne though I already knew that the promise of safe-conduct for me would be broken and that wild, strange treacheries and trickeries were being leveled against me. No matter how weak and inadequate I felt, my mind was firmly made up : Even if I knew that there were as many devils there as there were tiles on the roofs of Worms and all were taking aim at me, I would still come riding in.

On the way to Worms a herald asked me whether I still planned on going on to Worms. Although I was trembling, I answered : "I intend to go even if all the devils were there."

When Luther then was ordered to give a clear, simple answer as to whether he was prepared to recant or not, his final declaration was :
"Since Your Majesty and the gentlemen desire a simple answer, I will give it without intending to put teeth into it : Unless I am convinced by the testimony of Scripture or clear arguments (for I believe neither the pope nor the councils by themselves, as it is evident that they have often erred and contradicted themselves), I remain convinced by the Scripture passages that I have cited, for my conscience is bound by the Word of God. I cannot and will not retract anything, because it is neither safe nor sound to act against one's conscience." He closed his declaration, after an objection was raised and an uproar broke out in the audience, with the words : "God help me. Amen."

Kidnapping of Luther on the way back from the Diet of Worms

While Luther was on his way home from Worms, Elector Frederick the Wise arranged a fake capture of Luther. He planned it in order to keep him safe, even though the emperor had promised a safe-conduct to Luther for this journey. Already on May 25, 1521, he was put under the ban of the empire, so he was defenseless and exposed to every murderous attack.—Even today a memorial stone in the forest near Altenstein calls attention to this clandestine kidnapping of Luther.

Right: Memorial of Luther's capture

136

The Wartburg at Eisenach according to a copperplate from the year 1650

Even before Luther stayed at the Wartburg, this place had become widely known because of the landgravine of Thuringia, St. Elizabeth (1207—1231), and because of the minnesingers' poetic "War of the Wartburg" (1207).

Right: The Wartburg today

The Wartburg greets the wide countryside and each year attracts thousands of visitors from all countries of the world. Its importance lies not so much in its architectural beauty as in its being such a powerful historical symbol. Through Luther's stay there it has become a symbol of the Reformation.

138

Luther's study in the Wartburg in its present state

Luther devoted himself completely to intellectual activity during his 10-month stay at the Wartburg (from May 4, 1521, to the beginning of March 1522). His significant translation of the New Testament, completed here in two and a half months, was followed by other works: the "Booklet Concerning Confession," dedicated to Frank von Sickingen, who had also offered his castle to Luther as a refuge; a collection of sermons, "Portions of the German Church Postil"; and the treatise "On Monastic Vows," in which Luther condemned monasticism on Biblical grounds.

Right: The "Luther Hallway" on the upper floor of the residence

The solitude on the Isle of Patmos led the seer John to wrestle with God on behalf of the Christian churches; Luther regarded his captivity in the Wartburg as his "Patmos."

In the north court of the Wartburg

This architectural diversity in the north front yard together with the charming panel arrangements are impressive witnesses of Luther's "Squire George" days at the castle.

Chapel in the main building of the Wartburg. Present state

Today the Wartburg chapel is used by the Evangelical church for devotions and services.

People came on foot from Eisenach to meet and welcome us. Finally in the evening we arrived at Eisenach. Our companions continued on ahead with Jerome Schurf in the morning. I proceeded through the woods toward my relatives, who occupied practically the entire countryside, and I left them (Schurf and the others) as we turned in to Waltershausen. Soon afterwards I was captured near Altenstein. Amsdorf, of course, had to know that I was going to be apprehended by someone, but he does not know where I am being kept.

Luther as Squire George

Luther stayed at the Wartburg as "Squire George," continuing his work there; in the meantime his friends at Wittenberg carried out the Reformation of the church. Since they lacked competent leadership to cope with the threatening disturbances, Luther rode in disguise to Wittenberg already in December 1521. When the excitement of the populace nevertheless led to a wholesale destruction of images in February 1522, Luther's public appearance could no longer be delayed.

Charles V, German emperor, 1519—1556

In 1519 Spanish King Charles I was elected emperor of Germany. The election of this devoutly Catholic monarch threatened to bring a complete suppression of the Reformation. He wanted to restore the unity of the empire in the face of its internal and external foes. He was able to contain the impending Islamic invasion but not the new Evangelical faith in Germany.

146

Erasmus of Rotterdam, about 1466—1536

Also the humanists of the 15th and 16th centuries had a part in the intellectual preparation for the Reformation. Their leading representatives were John Reuchlin and Erasmus of Rotterdam. While the humanist Melanchthon very quickly embraced all of Luther's teaching, Erasmus severed his connection with it. Their disagreement found its expression in Erasmus' essay "On the Freedom of the Will" and in Luther's reply to it, "On the Bondage of the Will."

CHRISTO · SACRVM ·

ILLe · DEi · VERBO · MAGNA · PIETATE · FAVEBAT ·
· PERPETVA · DIGNVS · POSTERITATE · COLI ·

D · FRIDR · DVCI · SAXON · S · R · IMP ·
ARCHIM · ELECTORI ·
ALBERTVS · DVRER · NVR · FACIEBAT ·
B · M · F · V · V ·
M · D · XXIIII

148

John the Steadfast, elector of Saxony 1525—1532

Also the successor to Frederick the Wise clearly identified himself with the Reformation. When he was threatened with danger by the Catholic princes through the Dessau alliance, he concluded the Torgau Union with the young Landgrave Philip of Hesse to protect the Protestant territories against attack.

Left: Elector Frederick the Wise. Copper engraving by Albrecht Duerer

In spite of his personal reserve, Luther's sovereign, Elector Frederick the Wise, greatly furthered the Reformation by protecting Luther against the pope and the power of the emperor and by helping the Reformation to succeed in his own territory. The elector's commitment to Luther and his cause is the more remarkable when one considers that he and Luther never met or spoke to each other.

Philip of Hesse, 1509—1567

The young Landgrave Philip of Hesse enthusiastically championed the Lutheran Reformation. He called on the Protestant princes to form an alliance and in this way kept them from splitting up and being annihilated.

Luther and Huss distribute Holy Communion

The Reformation period recognized the very close connection between the "heretic" Huss and Luther, for Luther himself said of him : "John Huss was speaking of me when he wrote from Bohemia : 'Now they are going to roast a goose [in Bohemian *Husa* means goose], but a hundred years from now they will hear a swan sing, and they will have to bear it.'" In this contemporary woodcut Luther and Huss together are distributing Communion in the form of both bread and wine to the members of the Saxon elector's family. Luther, of course, was born more than a 100 years after Huss.

Grouping of reformers. Details from the epitaph of Mayor Meienburg by Luke
Cranach, Jr. Nordhausen, St. Blasius Church

We are indebted to the artists Luke Cranach (father and son) for practically all
pictures of the Reformation and its leading figures.—In the detail on the left
Luther occupies the center of attention, surrounded by Forster, Spalatin, and
Bugenhagen—in the one above we even find Erasmus of Rotterdam in addition
to Jonas, Cruciger, and Melanchthon.

153

Let us pray as we have done in the past, and God will hear us and do more than we ask, as He has done in the past; it would not hurt us especially to take our religion a little more seriously—and may He help us to do so—for we are about to face important and serious matters for which we need His great help in particular.

To Elector John Frederick; Wittenberg, August 21, 1542.

I, too, am truly sorry about that rift and certainly have also felt how harmful it is; I would gladly risk life and limb to restore harmony, if that were possible. If it weren't for my conscience, there would be nothing I would rather bear and do, but I cannot blot out my conscience forever, and remorse is like a gnawing worm in the heart.

To Landgrave Philip of Hesse; Wittenberg, December 17, 1534.

Huldreich Zwingli, 1484—1531

The humanist and priest Huldreich (Ulrich) Zwingli became a major force in the reformation of the German-speaking parts of Switzerland. He arrived at his reformation convictions independently of Luther but was influenced by Erasmus of Rotterdam. Luther's unwavering stand at the Leipzig debate strenthened his own religious convictions, and he now took up the battle against the antiquated ecclesiastical system. The rift between him and Luther over the nature of the Sacrament seriously weakened the forces of the Reformation camp, disunited as they now were.

The oldest preserved letter of Martin Luther,
written to his friend George Spalatin on August 5, 1514

In this letter Luther ridicules the presumption of a proofreader in a Cologne
printing firm who had attacked the famous humanist Reuchlin.—The letter is
now in the library of the Erfurt Evangelical Ministerium.

Luther's handwriting. A letter to Philip Rosenecker, T. D., at Jena

On the journey to Marburg, September 21—22, Luther had spent the night with Rosenecker and on the way home had preached in Jena on October 2d. This letter refers to one of Rosenecker's relatives, whose husband, Jerome Malter, had been captured in 1526. After three years she received a letter from her husband asking her to join him. Since she had married again in the meantime, Rosenecker asked Luther for advice.—The firm, clear hand of Luther is not difficult to read. The translation is as follows:

Grace and peace in Christ! My good friend: What I said to you in Jena about that marriage is still my opinion: Since Jerome Malter Buechsenmeister, her spouse, is still living and is with King Janus, she cannot with good conscience refuse to return to him. For King Janus is in league with the Turks, and so her husband is certainly safe. My advice, therefore, is that you or she write to the man and tell him everything. And beg him to forgive her and to take her back; in the meantime she should be separated and divorced from George and stay with you. When the man's answer arrives, we can decide what to do further. With this we commend you to God, Amen.

Thursday of St. Martin 1529   Martin Luther

157

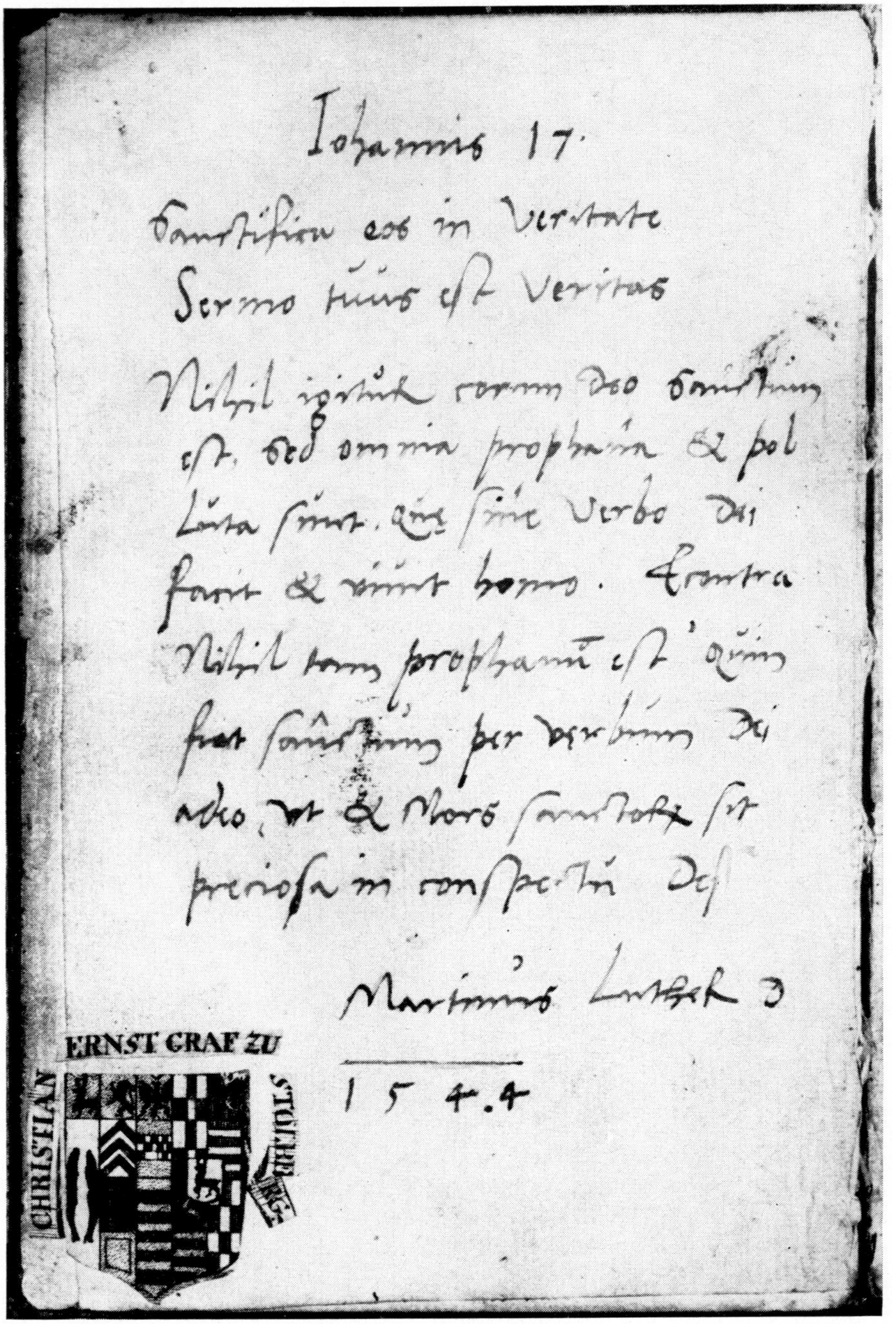

Iohannis 17.

Sanctifica eos in veritate
Sermo tuus est veritas

Nihil igitur eorum Deo sanctum
est, sed omnia prophana & pol
luta sunt, quae sine verbo Dei
facit & vivit homo. Contra
Nihil tam prophanum est, quin
fiat sanctum per verbum Dei
adeo, ut & Mors sanctorum sit
preciosa in conspectu Dei

Martinus Luther D

1 5 4 4

Martin Luther in the pulpit

The new teaching was portrayed by a great number of allegorical representations. Most frequently the new way in which Communion is celebrated was chosen. The Sacrament is no longer a supernatural sacrifice which the priest performs at the altar, but here Christ's body and blood "under the bread and wine" are offered to the believers for the forgiveness of sins.

Left: Martin Luther's handwriting from the year 1544

John 17, 17: "Sanctify them in the truth; Your Word is the truth." This is followed by Luther's own words: "There is nothing about them that is holy before God, but on the contrary, everything that man does and thinks without the Word of God is common and defiled. On the other hand nothing about them is common that is sanctified through the Word of God; even death becomes holy and precious in the eyes of God."

The Wittenberg City Church
In the foreground statues of Luther and Melanchthon

It was in the City Church of Wittenberg that the first Protestant Communion service *"sub utraque specie"* (i. e. the communicants received both bread and wine) was celebrated.—The Luther statue is by the famous sculptor Gottfried Schadow.

Luther pulpit

Luther's sermons had an immediacy and vitality about them which sprang from a profound knowledge of the Bible and his pastoral experience. Yet his final word bears evidence of a humility that almost puts us to shame: "Let no one think he has tasted enough of Holy Scripture until he has led the churches by means of prophets like Elijah, Elisha, John the Baptizer, Christ, and the apostles for at least a hundred years."—

Our picture shows the so-called Luther pulpit, now in Luther Hall in Wittenberg, from which Luther delivered many of his sermons.

Illustrations on pages 162 and 163:
Details of the Luther pulpit

I do not have a certain, special language of my own in German but use the common German language so that both High and Low Germans can understand me. I talk as they do in the Saxon chancellery, which all princes and kings in Germany follow ; all the imperial cities and the courts of the princes follow the form of writing used by the chancellery of Saxony and of our sovereign, and so it's the most common German language.

The German language is the most perfect language and has much in common with Greek. I thank God that I can hear and find my God in German in a way the very learned people (the Scholastics) have not found Him yet, neither in Latin, nor in the Greek or Hebrew tongue.

I have translated the New Testament into German according to the best of my ability and according to my conscience, but in doing so I have not forced anyone to read it ... ; no one is forbidden to prepare a better one ... It is my Testament and my translation, and it shall be and remain mine.

I wanted to speak German [in my translation] and not Latin or Greek, since I had undertaken to make a German translation.

Right : The Wittenberg Nightingale

The people's poet Hans Sachs also was one of Luther's ardent followers. His siding with Luther comes out in the song "The Wittenberg Nightingale," which goes : "Who is this lovely nightingale that sings the dreary night away and brings to us a bright, new day ? It's Martin Luther, that's the name, the monk from Wittenberg who came, and called us from that gloomy night which held us captive in its might."

164

Die Wittenbergisth Nachtigall
Die man yetz höret überall.

Ich sage euch/wa dise schweygē/so werdē die stayn schreyen Luce 19.

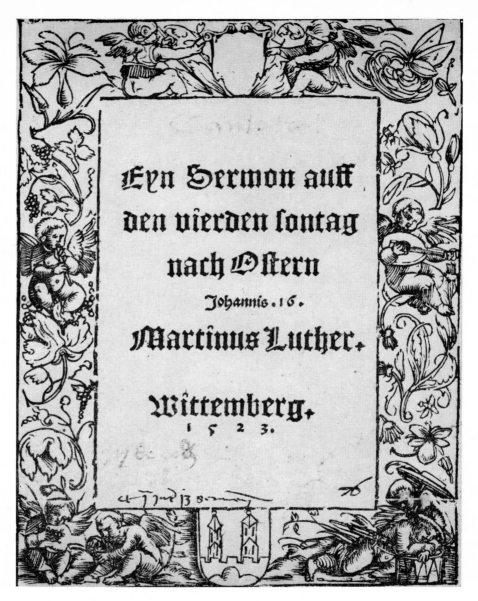

Eyn Sermon auff
den vierden sontag
nach Ostern

Johannis. 16.

Martinus Luther.

Wittemberg.
1 5 2 3.

Sermon for Cantate Sunday

Luther's sermons were passed from hand to hand, and his hymns were heard
before long in church, home, and school. These helped to break the ground for
the Reformation.

Enchiridion

Oder eyn Handbuchlein/

eynem yetzlichen Christen fast nutzlich
bey sich zuhaben/ zur stetter vbung
vnnd trachtung geystlicher ge-
senge/ vnd Psalmen/ Recht-
schaffen vnnd kunstlich
vertheutscht.

M. CCCCC. XXIIII.

❡ Ain ende dyses buchleins wyrstu fin-
den eyn Register/in welchê klerlich
angezeygt ist was vnd wie viell
Gesenge hieryn begriffen
sindt.

❡ Wie dyesen vnd dergleychen Gesenge
sollt mann byllich die inngenn
iugendt aufferzyhen.

Title page of the first Lutheran hymnbook, 1524.

John Gutenberg, about 1394—1468

John Gutenberg invented the art of printing with movable cast type. He set up the first printing press in Mayence; soon countless others followed in all cities of Germany. It was only his epoch-making invention that made possible the rapid spread of the Reformation ideas throughout all of the German lands.

Right: A page from the 42-line Gutenberg Bible

The greatest treasure from the early epoch of printing is Gutenberg's 42-line Bible, which came from his printing shop about 1452.

non fuiſſe auſum affirmare ſe raptū
in corpore ſed dixiſſe ſiue in corpore ſi
ue extra corp° neſcio deus ſcit. Hijs et
ralibz argumentis apopchas in li
bro eccleſie fabulas arguebat. Supra
qua re lectoris arbitrio iudiciū derelin
quens illud ãmoneo nou habeti da
nielem apud hebreos inter ꝓphetas:
ſed inter eos qui agyographa conſcri
pſerūt. In tres ſiquidē partes omnis
ab eis ſcriptura diuiditur: in legē in
prophetas et in agyographa id eſt
in quinꝗ et octo et undecim libros: de
quo nõ eſt huj° temporis diſſerere. Que
autē ex hoc ꝓpheta ꝓmo contra hūc
librū porphirius obiciat teſtes ſunt
methodi euſebius apollinaris: qui
multis verſuū milibus eius veſanie re
ſpõdētes neſcio an curioſo lectori ſa
fecerūt. Vnde obſecro vos o paula et
euſtochiū fundatis ꝓ me ad dñm pre
ces: ut quãdiu i hoc corpuſculo ſū ſcri
bã aliꝗd gratū vobis vate eccleſie: di
gnū poſteris. Preſentiū quiꝙ iudiciū
oblatantiū nõ ſatis moueor:ꝗ in utra
ꝗ partē aut amore labūt aut odio.

Incipit daniel ꝓphetis

ANno tercio regni io
achim regis iude ve
nit nabuchodono
ſor rex babilonis ihe
ruſalē et obſedit eã:
et tradidit dominus
in manu eius ioachim regē iude et parte
vaſorū domus dei: et aſportauit ea in
terrã ſennaar in domū dei ſui: et vaſa
intulit in domū theſauri dei ſui. Et
rex affatus eſt aſphero eunuchoꝝ ut intro
duceret de filijs iſrł et de ſemine regio
et tyrãnoꝝ pueros i quibz nulla eſſet
macula decoros forma et eruditos o
mni ſapiētia cautos ſciētia et doctos

diſciplina: et qui poſſent ſtare in pala
tio regis: ut doceret eos litteras et lin
guam chaldeoꝝ. Et conſtituit eis rex an
nonã per ſingulos dies de cibis ſuis
et vino unde bibebat ipſe: ut enutriti
tribus annis poſtea ſtarent in conſpectu
regis. Fuerūt ergo inter eos de filijs iu
de daniel ananias miſahel et azarias.
Et impoſuit eis ꝓpoſitus eunuchoꝝ
nomina danieli balthaſar: ananie
ſidrat miſahel miſac et azarie abde
nago. Propoſuit autē daniel in corde
ſuo ne polluretur de menſa regis neqꝫ
de vino potus eius: et rogauit eunuchoꝝ
ꝓpoſitū ne cõtaminaretur. Dedit autē de
us danieli gratiã et miſericordiam
in cõſpectu principis eunuchoꝝ. Et ait
princeps eunuchoꝝ ad danielē. Timeo
ego dñm meū regē qui cõſtituit vobis
cibū et potū: qui ſi viderit vultus veſtros
maciẽtiores pre ceteris adoleſcentibz
coeuis veſtris: condemnabitis caput
meū regi. Et dixit daniel ad malaſſar
quē cõſtituerat princeps eunuchoꝝ ſu
per danielē ananiã miſahelē et aza
riam. Tempta nos obſecro ſeruos tuos
diebus decem et dentur nobis legumina
ad veſcendū et aqua ad bibendum: et
cõtemplare vultus noſtros et vultus
pueroꝝ qui veſcuntur cibo regio: et ſi
cut videris facias cum ſeruis tuis. Qui
audito ſermone huiuſmodi tempta
uit eos diebus decem. Poſt dies autē de
cem apparuerūt vultus eoꝝ meliores
et corpulentiores pre omnibus pueris
qui veſcebãtur cibo regio. Porro ma
laſſar tollebat cibaria et vinū potus e
orum: dabatꝗ eis legumina. Pueris
autē hijs dedit deus ſcientiã et diſcipli
nam in omni libro et ſapiẽtia: danie
li aut intelligentiã omniū viſionum
et ſomnioꝝ. Completis itaqꝫ diebus

The printers are doing a very good thing by busily publishing good hymns and making them appealing by adding all sorts of embellishments, enticing people to see the joy of faith and to love to sing.

Of course, it is true that Christ has overcome the world. Then why do we tremble so before the conquered world as though it were the victor? It would be worth it to crawl on our hands and knees to Rome or Jerusalem to get such an assurance! But since we have texts like this by the thousands and are familiar with them, we do not think highly of them. That is not good. I know that this comes from weakness of faith; but let us pray like the apostles: "Lord, increase our faith!" (Luke 18, 5)

Right: Page from a handwritten Latin Bible

Formerly the Bible had to be copied laboriously by hand—a task performed primarily in the monasteries; now printed copies could be produced faster and more economically.

Initium euange[lii] ih[es]u [christ]i fi[lii] dei sicut s[crip]tum e[st] in y[saia] p[ro]ph[et]a Ecce mitto a[n]g[e]lu[m] meu[m] an[te] facie[m] tua[m] qui p[re]parabit uia[m] tua[m] an[te] te vox clamantis in deserto parate uia[m] d[omi]ni rectas facite semitas eius fuit iohes in deserto baptizans et p[re]dicans baptismu[m] penite[n]tie in re[m]issio[n]e[m] p[ecca]tor[um] Et egrediebatur ad eu[m] om[n]is iudee regio et ih[e]rosolimite uniu[er]si et baptizabant[ur] ab illo in iordanis flumi[n]e confitentes peccata sua Et erat iohes uestitus pilis came[l]or[um] et zona pellicea circa lumbos eius et locustas et mel siluestre edebat et p[re]dicabat dicens venit fortior me post me cuius no[n] su[m] dign[us] p[ro]cu[m]be[n]s soluere corrigia[m] calciamentor[um] eius Ego baptizaui uos aq[u]a ille u[er]o baptizabit uos sp[irit]u s[an]c[t]o Et factu[m] e[st] in die[bus] illis uenit ih[esu]s a nazareth gali[le]e et baptizat[us] e[st] a ioh[ann]e in iordane Et statim ascende[n]s de aqua uidit celos apertos et sp[iritu]m [tam]q[uam] colu[m]ba[m] descende[n]tem et mane[n]tem i[n] ip[s]o et vox facta est de celis tu es fili[us] meus dilectus in te co[m]placui Et statim sp[iritu]s expulit eu[m] in deser[tum] et erat in deserto q[ua]dragi[n]ta die[bus] et q[ua]dragi[n]ta noctibus et te[m]ptabat[ur] a sathana Eratq[ue] cu[m] bestiis et a[n]g[e]li ministrabant illi Postq[uam] aut[em] traditus e[st] iohes uenit ih[esu]s in galilea[m] p[re]dica[n]s euange[lium] regni dei dice[n]s q[uonia]m i[m]pletu[m] e[st] te[m]pus et ap[pro]pi[n]quauit regnu[m] dei p[e]nite[m]ini et credite euangelio Et p[re]terie[n]s secus mare galilee uidit symone[m] et andrea[m] fr[atr]em eius mitte[n]tes retia in mare erant e[n]im piscatores et dixit eis ih[esu]s uenite post me et facia[m] uos fieri piscatores ho[m]inu[m] et p[ro]ti[n]us relictis retibus secuti su[n]t eu[m] Et p[ro]gressus inde pusillu[m] uidit iacobu[m] zebedei et ioh[ann]em fr[atr]em eius et ip[s]os in naui co[m]pone[n]tes retia sua et statim uocauit illos et relicto p[at]re suo zebedeo in naui cu[m] mercen[n]ariis secuti su[n]t eu[m] Et ingrediu[n]tur capharnau[m] et statim sabbatis ingressus in synagoga[m] docebat eos et stupebant sup[er] doctrina eius erat e[n]im docens eos q[ua]si potestate[m] habens et no[n] sicut scribe Et erat in synagoga eor[um] ho[m]o in sp[irit]u i[m]mu[n]do Et exclamauit dice[n]s q[ui]d nob[is] et tibi ih[es]u na-

zarene an uenisti p[er]dere nos scio q[ui]a s[an]c[t]us dei Et co[m]minatus e[st] ei ih[esu]s dicens obmutesce et exi de ho[m]i[n]e Et discerpe[n]s eu[m] sp[iritu]s i[m]mu[n]d[us] et exclamans voce magna exiit ab eo Et mirati su[n]t om[n]es ita ut co[n]quirere[n]t int[er] se dice[n]tes q[ui]dna[m] e[st] hoc que[na]m e[st] doctrina hec noua q[ui]a i[n] potestate et sp[iritu]s i[m]mu[n]dis imp[er]at et obediu[n]t ei Et p[ro]cessit rumor eius statim in om[n]em regionem galilee Et p[ro]ti[n]us egredie[n]tes de synagoga uenerunt in domu[m] symonis et andree cu[m] iacobo et iohanne Decu[m]bebat aut[em] socrus symonis febricitans et statim dicunt ei de illa Et accedens eleuauit illa[m] app[re]he[n]sa manu eius et co[n]tinuo dimisit ea[m] febris et ministrabat eis Uesp[er]e aut[em] facto cu[m] occidisset sol afferebant ad eu[m] om[n]es male habe[n]tes et demo[n]ia habe[n]tes et erat om[n]is ciuitas cong[re]gata ad ianua[m] et curauit m[u]ltos q[ui] uexaba[n]t[ur] uariis languoribus et demonia m[u]lta eiciebat et no[n] sinebat ea loqui q[uonia]m sciebant eu[m] ip[su]m esse Et diluculo valde surgens egressus abiit in deserta[m] locu[m] ibiq[ue] orabat Et p[ro]secutus e[st] eu[m] symon et qui cu[m] illo erant Et cu[m] i[n]uenisse[n]t eu[m] dixer[unt] ei q[ui]a om[n]es querunt te Et ait illis eam[us] i[n] p[ro]xi[m]os uicos et ciuitates ut et ibi p[re]dice[m] ad hoc e[n]im ueni Et erat p[re]dicans i[n] synagogis eor[um] et i[n] om[n]i galilea et demonia eiciens Et venit ad eu[m] leprosus depreca[n]s eu[m] et ge[n]u flexo dixit i[m]ne si uis potes me mu[n]dare ih[esu]s aut[em] m[i]s[er]t[us] eius exte[n]dit manu[m] sua[m] et ta[n]gens eu[m] ait illi uolo mu[n]dare Et cu[m] dixisset hec statim discessit ab eo lepra et mu[n]datus est Et co[m]minatus ei et eiecit illu[m] et dicit illi uide nemi[n]i dixeris sed uade ostende te p[ri]nci[pi] sacerdotu[m] et offer p[ro] mu[n]datio[n]e tua que p[re]cepit moyses in testi[moniu]m illis Et ille egressus cepit p[re]dicare et diffamare serm[on]em ita ut ia[m] no[n] posset manifeste i[n] ciuitate[m] introire sed foris i[n] desertis locis esse et conueniebant ad eu[m] undiq[ue]

Et it[er]u[m] intrauit in capharnau[m] post dies octo Et audit[um] e[st] q[uod] in domo esset Et conuener[unt] multi ita ut no[n] caperet eos neq[ue] ad ianua[m] et loqueb[atur] eis v[er]bum et uener[unt] ad eu[m] fere[n]tes paralyticu[m] q[ui] a quat[u]or po[r]tabat[ur] et cu[m] no[n] possent offerre eu[m] illi p[re] turba nudauer[unt] tectu[m] ubi erat et patefacientes submiser[unt] grabatu[m]

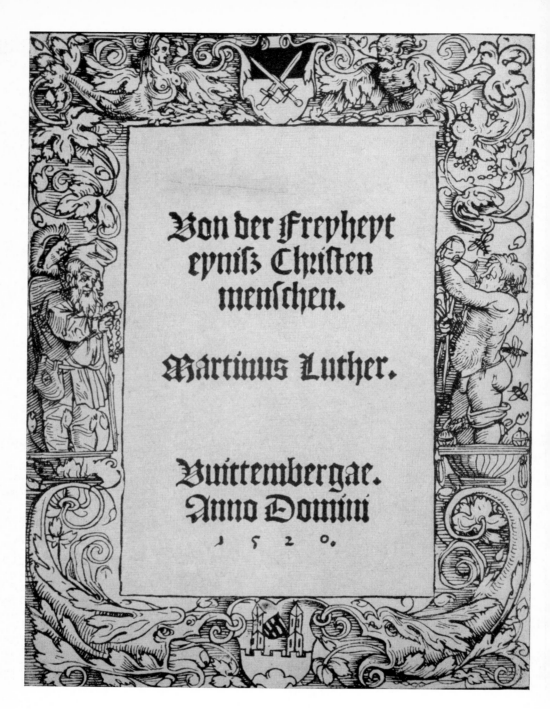

Von der Freyheyt
eyniß Christen
menschen.

Martinus Luther.

Vuittembergae.
Anno Domini
1520.

Left: Title page of "On Christian Liberty"

October 1520 marked the appearance of Reformation writings that freed the evangelical faith from all regimentation by old false doctrines. Luther begins this tract with this theme: "In order that we may thoroughly understand what a Christian is and what this liberty is all about which Christ has gained and given to a Christian and of which St. Paul writes so much, I am setting down these two guiding principles:

1. A Christian is a free lord over all and subject to no one (through faith),

2. A Christian is a bound servant of all and subject to everyone (through love)."

Luther's trademark in the Old Testament, about 1524

Since at Luther's time there were no copyright laws, Luther's writings were copied and sold without permission by many printers. Because these printers quite often were not very accurate, Luther had his trademark put on all editions commissioned by him; beneath it were the words: This trademark attests that these books have passed through my hands, for many are now making it their business to put out spurious copies and to ruin books. Printed at Wittenberg.

The Castle Church, view toward the chancel and tower

The Castle Church at Wittenberg is no longer dedicated "to all saints"; it has become a symbol of the Protestant Reformation. Luther's theses on the door of the church still exhort us: "When Christ our Lord says 'repent,' He means that the entire life of the believers on earth should be one of constant and unceasing repentence."

Interior of the Castle Church

The sovereigns and founders of the Castle Church, Elector Frederick the Wise and his brother John the Steadfast kneel at both sides of the altar. Martin Luther's tomb is underneath the pulpit at the side of the chancel.

I am going to speak the truth. I have suffered far greater anxiety than you will, I hope, ever experience ; and I have no desire to see anyone go through the same thing, not even those who rage against us now, no matter how great criminals and scoundrels they might be. And yet, even in such difficulties, I often found relief in the words of comfort spoken by a brother, perhaps you or Bugenhagen or Jonas or someone else. Since your turn has come, why don't you listen to us now? We certainly do not talk like carnally- and worldly-minded men ; you may be sure that we speak in the name of God through the Holy Spirit. Though we may be contemptible, let me tell you that He who speaks through us deserves no contempt.

To Melanchthon, Coburg, June 30, 1530

Luther writes to Melanchthon from Fort Coburg : "As far as the public controversies are concerned, I am only a carefree spectator," and he reveals the secret of his carefreeness by going on, "I faithfully stand by you with my sighs and prayers."

Right : Philip Melanchthon, 1497—1560

One of Luther's most intimate co-workers and friends was the outstanding university professor Philip Melanchthon. Having earned his M. A. already at 17, he came to Wittenberg as professor of Hebrew, Greek, and Latin in 1518. Under him the educational system was overhauled and the introduction of superintendents into the individual church districts decided upon. His most important work was the formulation of the Augsburg Confession, which was read as the confession of the Evangelical princes at the Diet of Augsburg in the presence of Emperor Charles V. Melanchthon lives on in history as "the teacher of Germany."

I really hate those deep anxieties by which you say you are being consumed. Not the greatness of the peril but the greatness of our unbelief is responsible for their dominating your heart. To Melanchthon, from Coburg, June 27, 1530.

I am praying for you, I have prayed for you, I will continue to pray for you, and I have no doubts about being heard ; for I can feel the Amen in my heart. Letter to Melanchthon, June 30, 1530.

Do what you can, as much as you can do at any given time with the proper means God has placed at your disposal, and remember that it is not possible to provide for every future contingency.

To Melanchthon, Wittenberg, October 24 or 25, 1544.

Melanchthon's dwelling on College Street in Wittenberg

Melanchthon's house—a gift of the elector—has been preserved in its original condition. In it Melanchthon also had a larger room available for lectures.— The building today houses the Melanchthon Museum.

179

IOHANNES LVFFT

Luther's publisher in Wittenberg was the well-known printer John Lufft.

Der sechs vñ dreyssigist psalm Dauid eynen Christlichen Menschen zu leren vñ trösten widder die Mütterey der Bößenn vnnd freueln Gleyßner.

Martinus Luther.
1521.

Printed title page of Psalm 36

The new art of printing now made it possible for Martin Luther's ideas to be propagated with lightning speed throughout the land and so contribute to very person's making his own decision about his religious convictions.

Ruins of the Nimbschen convent near Grimma

Katherine von Bora together with eight other nuns left the Cistercian convent on April 1, 1523, because they, too, were deeply stirred by the Reformation idea. —Today only the enclosure walls of the Nimbschen convent remain.—A plaque calls attention to Katherine's significant step.

In diesem Nonnenkloster weilte
1509-23
KATHARINA VON BORA.
Befreit wurde sie durch den Ratsherrn
Leonhard Koppe aus Torgau
am 1. April 1523.
Sie traf mit Dr. Martin Luther zu Wittenberg
am 13. Juni 1525.

Martin Luther, portrait by Luke Cranach, Sr., 1526

The great number of Luther pictures has never settled for historians the problem of what Luther really looked like. This portrait from the year 1526 is one of the few good pictures of Luther. True, it does not bring out the burning fire of his eyes "which," Luther's friends say, "blaze and sparkle like a star so that it is almost impossible to look into them," but the determined look of the reformer—here in the garb of a professor—is readily recognizable.

184

Katherine von Bora, portrait by Luke Cranach, Sr., 1526

"I would not trade my Katie for France or Venice because: (1) God has given her to me and me to her; (2) I often notice that other women have more faults than my Katie—although she has a few too, but they are balanced by far greater virtues; (3) she keeps the faith involved in marriage, which is faithfulness and honor."

Katey Luther's wedding ring

A fortunate turn of events has preserved the wedding rings of the Luther couple for posterity although the rings had become widely separated. Martin Luther's ring; once in the possession of the Dresden court, was given to the ducal house of Brunswick by August the Strong when he embraced Catholicism. Katherine's wedding ring changed hands many times before it found its home in the Leipzig City Historical Museum. The plain gold band (shown here inside the outer ring), which was the only ring worn by Luther's spouse, contains the Reformer's dedication and the date of the wedding: Martinus Lutherus, June 13, 1525. The highly embossed outer ring is a later addition from the same century. A crucifix and the instruments of Christ's torture form the relief work arranged around a mounted polished ruby.

The Luther goblet

King Gustav Vasa of Sweden, who introduced the Lutheran teaching into Sweden very soon after the Reformation started, presented this silver cup to Martin Luther in 1536 as a token of faithful adherence to him. It is a silver-embossed work, presumably of Scandinavian origin. It remained in the Luther family till 1613, then it passed from the hands of the grandson John Ernest Luther, canon in Zeitz, into the possession of the Leipzig city council. Even though the goblet had to be touched up many times in the course of centuries and though minor changes were made in the process, its shank which reminds us of organ pipes and has a Gothic frieze of foliage around it, is, at least, preserved in its original form.

Stone mug with the representations of Luther and Melanchthon

The heavy impact of the Reformation is still being reflected, also in areas which are not of a religious nature. The likenesses of Luther and Melanchthon were known everywhere and were widely circulated as woodcuts and engravings made from the portraits by Cranach and his school. They even found their way, among others, into the pottery workshops, where they were used as patterns for the relief ornamentation on the mugs and tankards popular in the 16th- and 17th-century taverns and city households. This tankard was made in the pottery city Kreussen (Upper Palatinate) about 1600. Certainly it must not have been a very common article, as the careful and elegant silver trim on the handle, base, and cover prove.

188

Luther's travel spoon

The Wartburg has in its possession a finely wrought spoon of gilted silver. Luther had given it for a present to his friend, John Caspar Aquila, who had helped him to translate the Old Testament.

The lower part has a somewhat round oval shape, the handle is short and stocky. Between the two is a caricature of the devil, which conceals a hinge for folding the spoon up. A picture of the crucified Savior is engraved in the middle of the bowl. Words from the Bible, in Hebrew and Latin characters, indicate the exalted meaning which the possessor had attached to this simple object.

View into the Luther room at Wittenberg

The Luther room has been kept in its original and simple form. Even today the large, colorfully glazed tile stove forms a special attraction.

Right: Interior of the Luther room

The bull's-eye window panes, the narrow seat in the window niche, the heavy old table, the colored paneling, all are eloquent witnesses of Martin Luther's "table talks."

192

Luther in his family circle. Painting by Gustav Adolph Spangenberg, 1866

Despite all the hostility and slander of those who were opposed to the Reformation, Luther married Katherine von Bora in the City Church of Wittenberg on June 13, 1525. The wedding celebration was held on June 27th in the former Augustinian monastery. Defying all kinds of scruples and worries, Luther founded a Christian home in which deep religious devotion, good times, and warm hospitality were a part of its greatest beauty.

*To my dear lady, Mrs. Doctor Martin Luther, voluntary martyr in Witten-
berg, into my gracious wife's own hands and humbly at her feet.*

Grace and peace in the Lord.

*Dear Katie, read John and the Small Catechism of which you once said :
"That book is talking all about me." You worry about your God as if He were
not almighty and could not create ten Martin Luthers if the old one should
happen to drown in the Saale river or get caught in the mouth of the oven or
in Wolf's fowling snare. Forget your cares, I have Someone who is far
better at taking care of me than you or the angels are. He is in a manger but
at the same time sits at the right hand of God the Father Almighty. So be
at peace. Amen.*   *Sunday after Dorothea's Day, Eisleben, February 7, 1546.*

*Peace lets us enjoy our life and limb, wife and child, house and home, yes,
all of our members, hands, feet, eyes, and our health and liberty ; surrounded
by this wall of peace we are safe. To have peace is certainly half of
Paradise. Peace can make a bite of bread taste like sugar and a drink of
water like Malmsey wine.*

*I cannot put up with those who despise music as all of our fanatics do. For
music is a gift and blessing of God. It also drives the devil away and makes
people happy ; it makes a person forget all anger, unchastity, pride, and
other vices. I put music next to theology in importance and respect it im-
mensely.*

*Music is the best gift of God. Oftentimes it inspired and stirred me so that
I again found pleasure in preaching.*

The Christmas hymn *Vom Himmel kam der Engel Schar* ("To Shepherds as They Watched by Night") in Luther's own handwriting

Lutheran hymnbook, Dresden 1625

Luther relief

This oldest representation of Luther in stone is affixed to the "Katherine portal" of the Luther House in Wittenberg. It bears the legend: "You shall find
strength in quietness and hope."

Right: The Luther rose

On the other side of the portal is Luther's coat of arms, also hewn in stone. The
inscription contains the first and final conviction of the Christian faith: "*Vivit—*
He lives!"
In referring to his coat of arms as a "badge of my theology," Luther himself wrote
these sentences which could serve as a summary of his whole Reformation doctrine:

198

"First there is a black cross set in a heart of natural color to remind me that faith in the Crucified One saves us. For if one believes from the heart, one is justified. Even though it is a black cross, one that mortifies the flesh and should produce pain, it leaves the color of the heart intact, does not destroy our nature, that is, it does not kill but preserves life. For "the just shall live by faith," but "by faith in the Crucified." This heart is mounted in the center of a white rose to show that faith brings joy, comfort, and peace. In short, faith transports us into a field of gay roses. Since the peace and joy are unlike that of the world, the rose is white and not red, for white is the color of spirits and all angels. The rose is set in a sky-colored field to show that such joy of the spirit and faith is the beginning of the heavenly joy to come, present, indeed, already in our joy now and embraced by hope, but not yet made manifest."

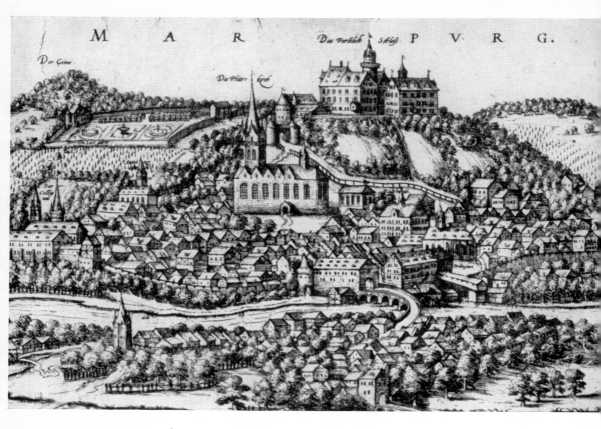

Marburg according to a copperplate by Braun and Hogenberg,
"Representation and Description of the Most Prominent Places in the World," 1582

In 1527 Philip of Hesse founded a university in his capital Marburg on the Lahn; this
was the first German university molded exclusively by Protestantism from the very
beginning.

Right: The subscribers to the Marburg Articles

In an attempt to settle the controversy between Luther and Zwingli, Philip of Hesse
arranged in October 1529 for a theological consultation in Marburg. Although complete agreement could not be achieved, the parties reached at least a partial understanding in the so-called Fifteen Marburg Articles. Justus Jonas, Philip Melanchthon,
Andrew Osiander, Stephen Agricola, and John Brentius had appeared with Luther
and John Oecolampadius, Martin Bucer, and Caspar Hedio with Huldreich Zwingli.

200

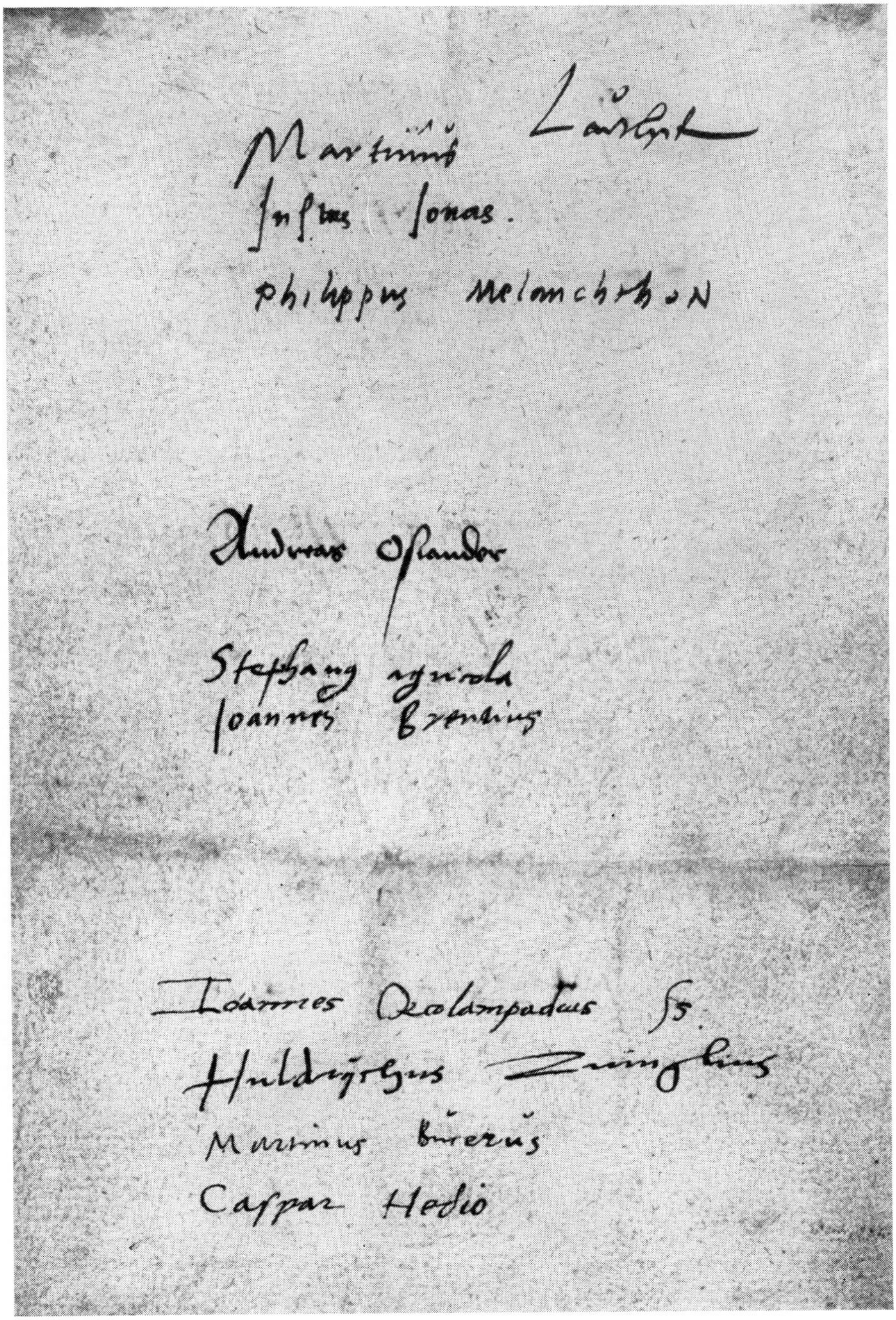

Martinus Luther

Justus Jonas.

philippus Melanchthon

Andreas Osiander

Stephanus agricola
Joannes Brentius

Joannes Oecolampadius ss.
Huldrijchus Zwinglius
Martinus bucerus
Caspar Hedio

Fort Coburg

Since Luther was under the imperial ban, he was not permitted to appear at the Diet of Augsburg (1530). From Fort Coburg—in order to be as close as possible to Augsburg—he tried to maintain contact with friends at the diet through numerous letters.

Memorial leaf to the Augsburg Confession

At the Diet of Augsburg the emperor wanted to settle the dispute with the Evangelicals. The *Confessio* drafted by Melanchthon did indeed contain many concessions of the Evangelicals but not the desired renunciation of the evangelical faith, so that reunion of the Evangelicals and the Catholics was not reached.

Gottes wort
bleibt ewig.

Biblia/ das ist/ die
gantze Heilige Sch-
rifft Deudsch.

Mart. Luth.

Wittemberg.

Begnadet mit Kür-
furstlicher zu Sachsen
freiheit.

Gedruckt durch Hans Lufft.

M. D. XXXIIII.

The advantage of having a German translation of the Bible is so great that no one even pays any attention to it. Nobody recognizes what great knowledge is offered by it to the world. What we once sought with great pains and by assiduous reading and still did not find is now offered to us by the exceeding clarity of the text itself, the meaning of which we could never have discovered in the obscurity of the old translations.

Translating into German requires great effort. For in translating the Bible into German we had to burn a lot of oil. But there will be some who will claim that they know better than we but who can't make a better one themselves. They will skin me for one little word when I could show them where they would be wrong in a hundred words if they were to translate. This will happen also to our faithful piece of work. If someone could translate only Psalms 72 and 73 into good German, I would give him 50 florins. But he would not be allowed to use any of our translation to do it.

Left: Printed title page of the first complete Bible ("Biblia, that is, the Entire Holy Scripture in German")

In the year 1534 John Lufft put out the first printing of the whole Bible in Luther's translation. Luther's Bible translation brought the development of the German language to a decisive turning point: from a great number of individual official German languages developed one common, German literary language.

Illustration on page 206: Luther's Small Catechism

In 1529 Luther's Small Catechism first appeared in a simple card form; afterwards the Large Catechism and the Small Catechism came out in book form. Up to this time only the priest said the Creed, now every child, after instruction in the Christian faith, could confess: "I believe that God has made me and all creatures . . ."

Der kleine Catechismus fur die gemeine Pfarr-herr vnd Prediger. Mart. Luther. Wittemberg.

John Bugenhagen, 1485—1558

Bugenhagen introduced the Reformation into Pommerania (where he hailed from) and other German territories. His talents equipped him for giving the proper external form to the new life which had sprung up. As architect of the various church orders he untiringly visited the parishes; as city pastor of Wittenberg he was Luther's faithful friend and father confessor.

Title page of the "German Mass and Order of Divine Service"

Right: Title page of "A New Hymnbook" printed in Leipzig, 1537

Ein New Ge=
sangbüchlin Geystlicher
Lieder/ vor alle gutthe
Christen nach or=
denung Chri=
stlicher kir
chen.

Ordenung vnd Gebrauch der
Geystlichen Lieder/ so in diesem bü=
chlin begriffen synt/ findest du am
ende diß Büchlins.

Ephe. 5.
Werdet voll des heyligen gey=
stes/ vnd redet vndereinander von Psalmen
vnd geystlichen Lobgesengen/ Synget lob
dem Herren in ewerm hertzen.

Gedruckt zu Leiptzigk durch
Nickel Wolrab.
1537.

THE EPITAPH

OF LENCHEN LUTHER,

THE YOUNG DAUGHTER

OF DR. MARTIN LUTHER

(PREPARED BY THE FATHER HIMSELF)

I AM ASLEEP AND WITHOUT FEAR,

SAYS LUTHER'S LENCHEN,

WHO LIES HERE;

WITH ALL THE SAINTS TO GLORY LED,

I REST HERE IN MY LITTLE BED.

FOREVER LOST I SHOULD HAVE BEEN

BECAUSE I WAS CONCEIVED IN SIN,

BUT NOW I LIVE, AND ALL IS GOOD,

FOR CHRIST

REDEEMED ME WITH HIS BLOOD.

Madeline Luther, d. 1542. Portrait by Luke Cranach, Sr.

The early death of his little daughter Madeline moved Luther very deeply, and only by trusting in a greater Father was he able to comfort the dying child: "Dear daughter, you have another Father in heaven; you are going to Him now."

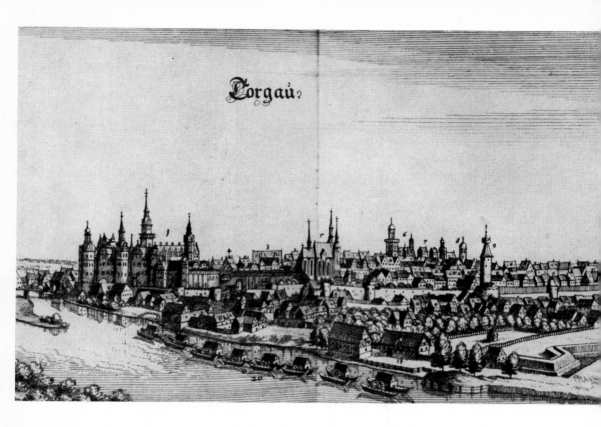

Torgau according to Merian's copperplate from the year 1650

This little city where the Saxon electors resided won a special place in the history of the Reformation because the Torgau Alliance (1526) of the Evangelical princes had been ratified here.

Right: Interior view of the Castle Church in Torgau

On October 5, 1544, Luther dedicated the Torgau Castle Church, the first newly built Evangelical church. In 1546 his dedication sermon was printed, in which he clearly outlines the evangelical conception of a house of God: "Thus the intention is clear: This house has been built and furnished in keeping with this spirit of liberty for the benefit of those who are here in the castle and at the court, or others who want to step in. We should not think of it as a special church, as though it were better than other buildings where God's Word is preached. In case of an emergency, when one might not want to, or could not, meet here, one could just as well preach at the well or anywhere else."

Luther's deathbed prayer : O my heavenly Father, God and Father of our Lord Jesus Christ, God of all comfort, I thank You that You have revealed to me Your dear Son Jesus Christ, in whom I believe, whom I have preached and confessed, whom I have loved and praised, whom the exasperating pope and all the wicked slander, persecute, and blaspheme. My Lord Jesus Christ, I commend my poor soul to You. O heavenly Father, even though I must now leave this body and be plucked out of this life, I know for certain that I will be allowed to stay with You forever and that no one can pluck me out of Your hands.

On February 16, 1546, in Eisleben, as the conversation at Dr. M. Luther's dinner table centered on death and illness, Dr. M. Luther said : "When I get back home to Wittenberg, I am going to lie down in a casket and let the maggots feed on a fat doctor." And in two days it came to pass that Doctor Martin Luther did die there in Eisleben.

Schubert: Reports on Luther's Death and Burial

The house in which Luther died in Eisleben

In 1546 Luther came to his native town once more, this time to settle an inheritance dispute among the Mansfeld counts. During his stay here, in the home of the town clerk, death overtook him. Was it premonition that caused him, while here, to autograph a book with the Bible verse: "He who keeps My Word shall never see death"?

214

Room and bed in which Luther died

In the cold sweat of death Luther made this last confession of his faith: "Into Your hands I commend my spirit; You have redeemed me, O God of truth. Yes, God so loved the world."

Luther's face in death

Right after Martin Luther died, a messenger on horseback went to Halle and brought the painter Furttenagel to make a portrait of the face of the deceased. It almost seems as if these eyes had closed only in sleep, ready to open again in the next moment and bring new life into the face.

No one can understand ·Vergil's pastoral poems unless he has been a shepherd for five years.

No one can understand Vergil's poems about farming unless he has been a farmer for five years.

No one can completely understand Cicero's letters unless he has been active in important political affairs for 20 years.

Let no one think he has had enough of Holy Scripture until he has governed the churches with prophets like Elijah and Elisha, with John the Baptizer, Christ, and the apostles for 100 years.

Do not lay a hand on that divine Aeneid (Holy Scripture), but follow in its footsteps in humble adoration.

It is true, we are beggars.

After Luther's death these words were found on a slip of paper lying on his table.

Transporting Luther's remains to Wittenberg

Luther's remains were transported in a solemn, armed procession from Eisleben through Halle and then to Wittenberg. The rector of the university, the professors, students, and the city council together with many citizens met the funeral procession at the city gates and followed it to the Castle Church to pay their last honors to the deceased Reformer.

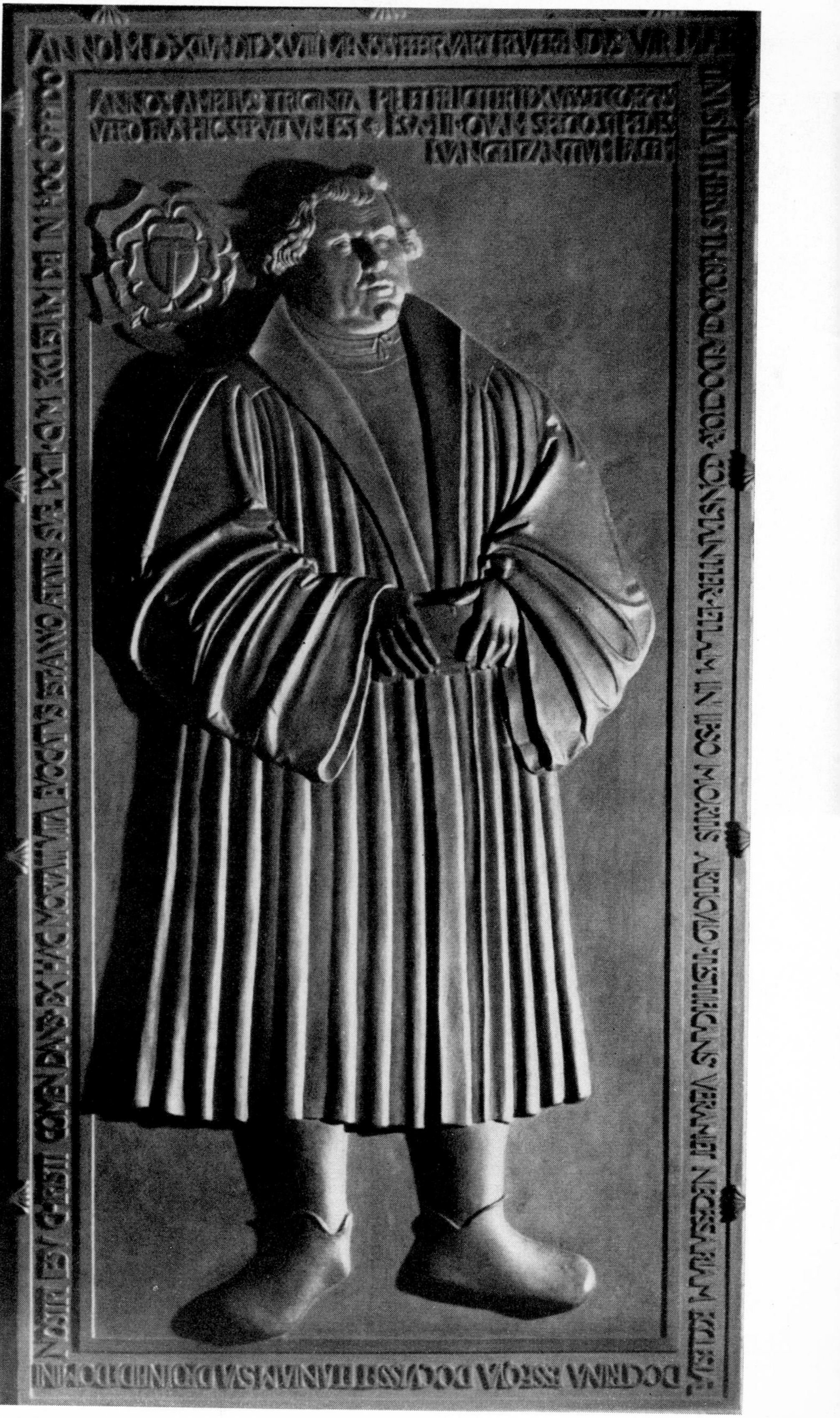

Luther's grave in the Castle Church

Dr. Martin Luther found his last resting place in the Castle Church at Wittenberg. The cover plate on his grave is as plain and simple in design as was the external course of his tension-filled life.

Left: Copy of the grave plate

The original epitaph which had been planned for Luther's grave was cast in Thuringia. However, the disorders attending the wars which broke out afterLuther's death prevented its transportation to Wittenberg. Up to now the original has remained in Jena; the one placed in the Castle Church at Wittenberg is only a cast of the original.

HE DIED IN THE YEAR 1546,

AT THE AGE OF 63 YEARS

AS HE WAS ENTERING HIS 64th YEAR.

HE DIED DURING

THE NIGHT OF FEBRUARY 18th

BETWEEN TWO

AND THREE O'CLOCK·

AND WAS BURIED

IN WITTENBERG

ON THE 22d OF THE SAME MONTH.

AND EVEN THOUGH HE

BE DEAD—HE LIVES.

The Reformer shortly before his death. Likeness by his famulus Reifenstein and handwritten text by Melanchthon. Translation on page 222.

Photos and reproductions were made available by: Adam, Erfurt, Page 107; A. Bayr, Erfurt, 97; W. Danz, Halle, 104/105, 186, 215, 216; Deutsche Fotothek, Dresden, 68, 69, 71, 96, 123, 129, 138, 147, 155, 157, 159, 165, 168, 172, 173, 184, 185, 202, 203, 213; M. Etzold, Leipzig, 189; Gewitz, Eisenach, 85; Gofferjé & Vollhaber, Erfurt, 89, 91, 92, 93, 94, 98, 99, 102, 156; W. Kirsch, Wittenberg, 161, 162, 163; A. Krahmer, Erfurt, 100; Museum der bildenden Kuenste, Leipzig, 192, 193, 194; Foto Marburg, Bildarchiv, 201; W. Remd, Graefenau-Angstedt, 81; Staatl. Museen, Berlin, 152, 153; G. Uhlmann, Leipzig, 67; Wartburgstiftung, Eisenach, 139, 140, 143, 150, 188; W. Wolf, Goerlitz, 141. All other photos were supplied by the authors.